THE
ACCOMPLISHED WOMAN

THE
ACCOMPLISHED WOMAN

12 Steps to Redefine
Success and Live Life
on Your Own Terms

CHRISTINA TRACY STEIN, PhD

Published 2025 by Gildan Media LLC
aka G&D Media
www.GandDmedia.com

THE ACCOMPLISHED WOMAN. Copyright © 2025 by Christina Tracy Stein. All rights reserved.

No part of this book may be used, reproduced or transmitted in any manner whatsoever, by any means (electronic, photocopying, recording, or otherwise), without the prior written permission of the author, except in the case of brief quotations embodied in critical articles and reviews. No liability is assumed with respect to the use of the information contained within. Although every precaution has been taken, the author and publisher assume no liability for errors or omissions. Neither is any liability assumed for damages resulting from the use of the information contained herein.

Front cover design by David Rheinhardt of Pyrographx
Front cover author photograph by Geri-Ann Galanti

Interior design by Meghan Day Healey of Story Horse, LLC

Library of Congress Cataloging-in-Publication Data is available upon request

ISBN: 978-1-7225-0727-5

10 9 8 7 6 5 4 3 2 1

This book is dedicated to my husband Damon and our children Julia, Will, and Scarlett. My greatest joy comes from our adventures together and our quiet moments of connection.

And to all the incredible accomplished women in the world. Some of you are my family, some of you are my friends, some of you I've yet to meet, but all of you are making a meaningful difference in your own way and I'm grateful to be on this journey with you.

Contents

Introduction 9

Chapter 1
Define Success for Yourself in Every Area of Your Life 15

Chapter 2
The Power of Clarity and the Process of Setting Goals 37

Chapter 3
Build Your Confidence, Overcome Self-Doubt,
and Cultivate Resilience 61

Chapter 4
Have the Courage to Express Yourself, Communicate Clearly
and Connect Authentically with Others 81

Chapter 5
Harness Your Unique Value and Find Purpose
in Everything You Do 111

Chapter 6
Redefine Success in Motherhood 129

Chapter 7
Your Relationships Determine the Quality of Your Life 149

Chapter 8
You Matter: Prioritize Your Health and Well-Being 173

Chapter 9
Improve Your Relationship with Money and Become Financially Empowered 193

Chapter 10
Master Your Time and Energy to Achieve Life Balance 221

Chapter 11
Never Stop Investing In Yourself: The Power of Being a Lifelong Learner 243

Chapter 12
Design Your Legacy and Live a Meaningful Life 267

Conclusion
You Are an Accomplished Woman 283

About the Author 295

Introduction

IN THE EARLY EIGHTIES, around the same time I was born, my father, Brian Tracy, recorded an audiocassette program designed to empower and inspire women in their careers and on their path to success. At the time, the circumstances and possibilities for women in the workplace were not nearly as bright or broad as they are today.

Fast-forward to the nineties, when my dad updated the program and built it into a seminar titled "Peak Performance Woman." It was based on three key questions:

1. What was "success" to the modern nineties career woman?
2. What were the obstacles to success most commonly faced by these women?
3. What did women need to learn to achieve greater success and deal with the obstacles that appeared to stand in their way?

At the time, the biggest obstacles women faced were office politics and the fact that the work environment was biased towards men. These women had to fight for recognition, opportunities for advancement, and promotability. In order for a woman to be taken seriously and respected by colleagues, she had to dress like men and step into her masculine power to demonstrate her worthiness for respect. Often that meant committing to her career at the sacrifice of relationships and family in order to show she was serious and valuable assets to a business. Success was measured in paychecks and titles.

Ambitious women of the nineties worked hard to achieve professional success, but they also wanted to experience peace of mind, balance, a freedom from guilt, economic freedom and self-reliance, equal access to opportunities, influence, self-confidence, and control of their work life and ability to achieve results. Although these women are not dissimilar to the women of today, the definition of success has evolved, and what women want now encompasses much more.

Which brings us to the present and yet another opportunity to update and explore the question of how the modern woman describes success. Or, as I like to say, what makes her feel like an accomplished woman?

Before we go on, let me tell you a little bit about myself, my father, Brian, and how this book came to be. Brian Tracy is a pioneer in personal and professional development. He has spoken to more than a million people in eighty-six countries and has published over 100 books on human potential, success, sales, and time management. I grew up watching him teach people how to achieve success, and I benefited from hearing all of his lessons around personal growth, focus, and goal setting.

I was born in 1980, so by the time he created "Peak Performance Woman" in the nineties, I was still a child in elementary school. But human potential was in my blood. As I grew up, I became passionate about psychology and personal and professional development. I decided to pursue my own career path in becoming a marriage and family therapist and later getting my PhD in human sexuality, focusing on intimacy and relationships. My goal has always been to help people discover and develop their dreams to achieve professional success while building and maintaining meaningful relationships.

My father and I have worked together in many ways over the years, and together we have coauthored three books on personal and professional development. We have had many conversations about the different issues people face—his view from a business perspective and mine from more of an interpersonal and emotional one. Our work bridges generations, blending his proven techniques with my expertise, coupled with our shared passion for teaching others to communicate effectively through speaking, writing, and coaching.

I appreciate collaborating with my dad partly because he is a traditional man with a strong masculine voice. When I say "traditional," I mean he grew up in a time where men were the breadwinners and women were the homemakers. He has taken pride in being a good provider and taking care of my mother and our family. Don't get me wrong: I also grew up with a father who taught me that I could do anything I wanted to do as long as I was willing to work for it. Of course, he'd hoped I'd marry a good guy who was hardworking and successful, but his message was clear: my potential was limitless.

When he and I collaborate and discuss professional topics, it is helpful for me to hear and integrate his traditional masculine voice with my more contemporary feminine voice. It has been interesting to hear his perspective on a given subject as it relates to men versus mine as it relates to women. This is especially true about women pursuing their profession while striving to maintain balance in life.

In 2013, Sheryl Sandberg wrote *Lean In: Women, Work, and the Will to Lead*. At the time, I was a young mother with three young children. I remember speaking with my dad about how I felt reading her book. She emphasized how women who wanted to achieve professional success needed to lean in and fully show up in their professional environments in order to demonstrate their commitment and show that they were worthy of recognition and promotion.

As a woman who felt committed to my role as mother and wife as well as having professional ambitions, I felt very frustrated. I did not like the idea that in order to achieve success, I had to sacrifice my desire to be a present mother and loving wife. It became clear to me that there was no one way to achieve success. Each individual had to define for themselves what would make them feel accomplished and balanced in their lives.

Which brings us to this book. By focusing on twelve main areas, I have set out to redefine the traditional definition of success for the modern woman to include a balance of professional ambitions, family aspirations, and personal fulfillment. Women's lives today are much more complex than they were when my dad's original programs were developed in the eighties and nineties. I believe that the desire for and achievement of living a life with purpose, balance, and fulfillment are the new pillars of success. In my experience, most women are ambitious and passionate. They are excited to use their gifts to contribute to their homes, jobs, and community in their own unique ways.

In the following chapters, you'll discover practical skills and guidance to help you succeed on your own terms, at your own pace, and in multiple areas of your life, whether you are navigating the difficult balance of motherhood and career or stuck navigating significant roadblocks. Each chapter will explore one of twelve areas that I've identified as significant aspects for holistic success and feeling accomplished. At the end of each chapter, you'll learn the essential steps you need to take in order to build confidence, feel empowered, and take action to achieve both professional goals and personal ambitions. I'll even share lessons I learned from my dad and insights from my own personal journey, revealing key transformations and lessons from my growth that you can apply to yourself.

Chapter 1
Define Success for Yourself in Every Area of Your Life

My father was and is passionate about positive psychology and how to build self-esteem. He took parenting very seriously, and as the firstborn child, I believe I got the biggest dose of "I really want to do this right." When I was growing up, I remember that almost every time he saw me, he would light up and say something like, "There she is." He made me feel I was one of the most important things in the world to him, and I must admit it felt good believing I was so special.

He was good at telling me how proud he was of me and that he believed I was a "remarkable young woman." As I reflect on my childhood, I realize that one of the things he had learned was that if you tell someone something, they start to believe it and it shapes how they view themselves. If someone tells you how great you are, you start to think you might actually be great. The same is true if you get negative feedback from the people around you. Fortunately or unfortunately, we believe what we are told.

Since my dad was so generous in his praise and seemed to believe that I was incredible, I grew up feeling driven to be "remarkable." I wanted to do and be something that was impressive and deserved the title that I had been given.

However, I also grew up watching my mother embrace her role as wife and mother. I would often ask her about her own ambition, and she would tell me how much she supported my father and believed in his work. She supported him in many ways and dedicated herself to our home and being his pillar of strength. Her dedication in running the family and managing all the behind-the-scenes details of his life made his contributions possible. He could not have done the work he has done without her; that has been her choice, her way of feeling accomplished. It is a choice that many women make: they are often the unsung heroes of their partner's great success.

So I grew up with two very different models of success: (1) chart a new course and become a pioneer that changes the world (yeah, I know: a high bar), or (2) embrace a traditional role and dedicate yourself to your family as a mother and wife.

I couldn't wait to get married and have kids. I didn't spend all those hours playing with dolls and pretending to not to get to do it for real. However, the concept of having my own ambition and the desire to do something "bigger" was equally as strong. I love my mom, but from my perspective, I feel she had more to offer and was way too generous in her sacrifice.

I've come to realize that feeling accomplished is a deeply personal thing. It's based on each woman's idea of her own life and what matters to her in each facet of her world. I admit I have judged my mother for what I believed to be "settling," but I also have come to appreciate that my path is mine alone, just as her path is hers. If I want others to see my contributions and honor how I have come to feel accomplished, I also need to respect and honor how other women have come to feel accomplished. At the core, every woman must do what has the most meaning for her and not for anyone else.

To embrace your own path and live a life of meaning and purpose, it is helpful to understand the historical perspectives and narratives that have influenced the experience of success for women who came before us, as well as the unique pressures that women face today.

As modern women, we face the challenge of navigating our professional ambitions, our desire to have a family, and the societal expectations of doing everything and being everything. It is not about getting permission from the world around us: it's about deciding what you want and who you want to be and confidently stepping into yourself. You get to reflect, redefine, and align your vision of success with what truly fulfills you, not what you think others expect of you.

Deconstructing the Script

Where you are right now is the result of your unique experience and the influence of your family, your friends, and the community you grew up in, as well as your education and the media you were exposed to. All of these have contributed to your attitudes and values.

Our self-concept, the way we view ourselves, is like a garden: throughout our lives, different ideas, values, and beliefs are planted in it. Our garden is filled up with other people's ideas about who we are and who we should be. To move forward and live your life authentically, you need to decide which plants and flowers you want to keep and embrace, and which plants don't serve you and are weeds that need to be pulled.

Think of all the different narratives you heard about women when you were growing up. How many of those did you absorb into your view of yourself and the world?

The only way to redefine what success means to you is to explore your garden and discover what ideas contribute to your self-concept. (Later I will introduce you to an exercise that will help you "weed" your garden). Those ideas are a part of a long history of expectations and beliefs about success for women. We need to explore those historical perspectives, the modern challenges women face, and the ever-evolving nature of what matters and when.

Historical Perspective

I recently had a conversation with my mother. She shared with me how when she was growing up in the fifties and sixties, her mother tried to keep up with the expectations for women at that time. They were expected to be dedicated homemakers who managed the house and cared for the children. In fact, keeping a tidy house was such a focus for these women that they had official competitions around who did the best job housecleaning. If you were lucky enough to win one of these competitions, you would benefit from a new vacuum cleaner or other handy household cleaning item. During these competitions, they would even investigate the cupboards and check for dust hidden in the back.

By the late sixties, many women were so bored with their household chores that when Valium (otherwise known as "mother's' little helper") came onto the market, it brought much-needed relief to women who were dealing with the stress of juggling the demands of motherhood and home life. Valium was just the thing to take the edge off (even though a lot of women ended up dependent on this and other drugs).

Not every woman was limited to a household role. This was also a time when women could work outside the home, although their options were limited to "feminine" jobs like nursing, teaching, or being a secretary (as in the television series *Mad Men*). Still, the overall societal expectation was that women should focus on the home, always appear put together, and behave "appropriately."

The seventies brought a huge shift for women with the rise of the feminist movement. Women had increased access to education and were able to pursue certain professional degrees, which opened new career paths. With more opportunities (still limited, of course) than they had had before, they still had to fight gender biases around equal pay, access to leadership roles, and domestic responsibilities. Women had access to birth control and could make choices around marriage and motherhood in a whole new way.

Of course, the woman who pursued a career outside of the home and wanted to also have a family still needed to find balance and navigate all of her responsibilities. This was a time when women had greater control of how they could invest their time and energy and pursue professional ambitions and personal lives. Reproductive rights, education, and career opportunities opened the door to a major shift for women.

These developments introduced a new wave of expectations and pressure for women. Yes, you could work and pursue your career, but your choices might result in feelings of judgment and guilt. Women moved out of a collective box of strictly being homemakers and were distributed into three categories: the woman who continued the role of traditional wife and mother, the childless career woman, and the woman trying to balance both.

> **Different Tracks for Women**
> 1. Traditional wife and mother
> 2. Career woman with no children
> 3. The woman trying to balance both

The pressure to "have it all" was the theme of the eighties for women. They were expected to pursue a professional job, often in a male-dominated field, where they fought to earn respect (thank you shoulder pads and "power dressing"). They were still fighting for gender equality in the workplace and society, challenging traditional roles and domestic responsibilities and voicing their desire for equal opportunities. At the same time, they were supposed to be equally successful as mothers and wives, continuing to keep a clean, organized house and having dinner on the table at the end of the day. The pressure to fully show up in each context made it very challenging to achieve balance.

The nineties was a big decade of progress for working women and really turned the tides when it came to claiming more opportunities personally and professionally (go, "girl power").

In increasing numbers, women were elected to political office in the U.S. Senate and House of Representatives. Janet Reno became the first woman to serve as U.S. attorney general. Laws were passed to award women financial and retirement security and The Family and Medical Leave Act of 1993 protected women from being fired for taking maternity leave. In 1991, almost two thirds of married women with children worked and provided significant amounts to the family's income—in many cases, contributing more than their spouses. Women also increasingly claimed independent identities outside of the home, choosing to delay marriage and children to pursue higher education and professional roles that had been unavailable to their mothers.

If the nineties launched women forward, the 2000s expanded how they claimed their own personal identities and definitions of achievement.

If the nineties launched women forward, the 2000s expanded how they claimed their own personal identities and definitions of achievement. We saw women in high-level corporate jobs, stay-at-home moms cultivating their social networks, and individuals with unique talent and ambitions in fields like art, entertainment, and sports. More women achieved leadership roles and were recognized as successful and influential within different industries and communities. The empowered women of the 2000s presented themselves with confidence, personal style, and conviction. We saw the transformation of women like Oprah Winfrey from talk show host to major media mogul and philanthropist. We watched Hillary Clinton go from first lady to the first female presidential candidate nominated by a major party. Women like Serena Williams, the record-breaking tennis player, and actress Angelina Jolie used their platforms to inspire and influence others.

With all this progress, a great majority of women continued to traverse the challenge of having a successful career and a stable, rewarding family life. Even though they achieved greater financial security and social recognition, finding the balance between work and home remained a common but often elusive goal.

Here we are in the year 2025. It remains important to each of us to feel like an accomplished woman, and what matters varies across many areas of a woman's life. Women of today are seeking achievement and success not just through career advancement, holding significant leadership roles, or financial independence: there is also great emphasis on going beyond traditional ideas of "work" success. Women want to honor their authentic selves and in so doing, they pursue passions, try to make a difference in the world, contribute to social change, and prioritize well-being. There is a great deal of opportunity to make an impact by becoming advocates, promoting causes, and empowering others.

Even so, those three boxes from the seventies still exist. There are women who proudly choose to be stay-at-home mothers and wives; women who decide to focus on their careers; and women who strive to excel in their chosen field while successfully managing a rewarding homelife. Beyond the general question of "What do you do with your time?" women have embraced the idea that personal fulfillment, self-care, and self-advocacy are the foundation of a successful life. What is built on top of that foundation will be different, although it will be equally valuable in the eyes of each builder.

Modern Challenges and Opportunities

Women today have so many choices. With all these options comes the fear of making the wrong decision or feeling guilty about the choice you've made. It's human nature to want to fit into the social group around you, and if you have chosen to act in a way unlike that of your peers, you may have a feeling of being on the outside. Social media, which enable us to see much of the lives of others, makes it even harder to avoid comparing yourself to other women and further questioning your choices.

With my first child, I subscribed to the attachment parenting style, which embraces "baby wearing" and nursing until the age of two. I was the only one in my mommy peer group doing this, and even though I had made the choice for our family, I still felt self-conscious about my decision.

Mothers who choose to work full-time struggle with not being able to volunteer in their child's class or be there for every school event. Women who choose not to have children may feel the judgment of other women, who see their choice as selfish.

Women need to support other women, encourage them, and empower them to achieve success for themselves. The last thing any woman needs is to balance her own quest for personal fulfillment and self-discipline with the external pressure of social acceptance and fear of being ostracized. It's important to accept that what is right for you might not be right for someone else, but if you give a woman space to be herself, you can earn that same respect. Remember, we are not the same, and in our different ways of providing value, we collectively improve the lives of everyone. As the nineteenth-century thinker Robert Ingersoll observed, "We all rise by lifting others."

We all rise by lifting others.

We are living in a fast-changing world. No matter what track you pursue to achieve success, you will be faced with the need to adapt and course-correct in the light of new information. Your ability to balance the responsibilities in your life and manage your time in a way that keeps you focused on what is important to you will determine what you can achieve.

There are many options for women today. Yes, there are obstacles within those options, but if you know what you want, the challenge is not a lack of opportunity but the lack of self-discipline and conviction in your pursuits.

Changing with the Time

As I write this, I'm almost forty-five years old. I've been married for twenty years, and I have three children. I've pursued a profession in psychology and focused my career on empowering people both personally and professionally. My definition of an accomplished woman has been strongly influenced by my phase of life. I remember being eighteen years old and getting ready to go off to college. I had big plans, but I was focused on professional ambition. I wasn't concerned about the well-being of my unborn children or the quality of my relationship to my future husband. I didn't think about how I could contribute to my community or make a lasting impact in society. Self-care was a foreign concept. My view of the world had not yet expanded.

I say this because you will go through this book and learn about important concepts and actionable skills that you can apply now, no matter what stage you are at. Nonetheless, how you define success will change throughout your lifetime, and that's OK.

I recently had a conversation with a dear friend who shared with me how she had gone to a prestigious college and then pursued a career in advertising. She was recognized for her talent and was very successful. When she got married, she continued to work, but when she had her son, everything changed. She felt that the most important thing she could do was to be a dedicated mother to him and focus on her role as mother and wife. She fully embraced this definition of success and used her talents in ways that aligned with her choice: she became active with the PTA at his school and organized book groups for him and his peers. Now he is about to go off to college, and she will yet again have an opportunity to redefine success. She can evaluate each area of her life and decide what it will take for her to feel accomplished now. Some ideas will remain the same, but others will evolve, and that is the nature of this process.

Give yourself permission to make decisions about your life right now, in the phase you are in, so you can define success for yourself, set goals, and take action moving toward those ideals. Commit to reevaluating this process in the future, and see what changes and what remains the same.

Unique Pillars of Success

As we move away from the traditional definition, which limits success to what a woman achieves professionally and how much money she earns, we move toward a more holistic view of success. This encompasses professional ambitions, family aspirations, and personal fulfillment. We consider living with purpose, feeling fulfilled, and balancing responsibilities.

To define success for yourself, you need to reflect and identify the current attitudes, values, and beliefs you have in every area of your life. In that way, you can determine if they accurately represent who you are and who you want to be. Only then can you use them as an accurate guide for setting goals and defining achievements.

Your Career and Ambition

When you were growing up, what did important women in your life do with their time? What was your family's attitude about women working and earning money? How did that shape your idea of pursuing a career or ambition?

When you were growing up, what did important women in your life do with their time?

How would you know if you were successful in your career or in pursuing your ambition? For many women, it would be measured by titles and paychecks, but it's important to think beyond that. How do you feel about your work, the contributions you make, and the way you serve others?

I believe strongly that every person comes into this world with a unique talent or skill and that when we discover that talent and use it to serve others, we unlock our potential in a powerful way. We will talk more about this in a later chapter, but for now ask yourself if the work you do or want to do inspires you and affords you the opportunity to really make a difference. Are you doing work that fulfills you and reflects your own unique sense of purpose?

You may have no desire to pursue a traditional job. You get to define what success in this area is for you. You may want to volunteer or pursue a creative ambition. You may choose to be a homemaker and embrace the role of mother and spouse. As long as you feel fulfilled by your choice, you can excel at it.

Money and Accomplishment

One of my biggest motivators for writing this book was to explore the topic of money as it relates to feelings of accomplishment. I grew up believing that the more money you made, the more valuable you were, and I've spent many years exploring the topic and my own relationship with money. I've gone from depending on my parents to depending on my husband to earning enough money that I can depend on myself.

I know this topic is very emotional for most people and isn't always discussed openly. I want you to explore your relationship with money and connect to where your ideas come from. Who earned the money when you were growing up? Who decided how that money was spent? What were the attitudes and beliefs around money? Was it merely a tool, or did it carry some emotional weight? Was money used as love or withheld for control? Did you receive an allowance, or did you never have enough for what you wanted? Did you work for money, or was it given to you?

Decide what you want your relationship with money to look like in the future. It is one of the most important relationships you have. It determines how you spend, how you save, and how you value your efforts, both personally and professionally. It will also influence how you interact with others.

Traditionally—and it's a view that is still prevalent today—the value of something is measured by how much someone else is willing to pay for it. This attitude has been especially challenging for women, who often work very hard on important things that don't result in a paycheck. For example, being a mother is one of the hardest jobs in the world, but no one gets a paycheck for that. To change that script for yourself, either embrace the value you offer without needing financial recognition or confidently demand compensation for the value you offer.

Relationships

Personal relationships nurture our well-being. Cultivating those meaningful connections can boost your confidence and support you to pursue your passion and goals. Studies have shown that the happiest people are those who contribute to others and feel that they are part of a group larger than themselves. This could be your family, your friends, a community you are involved in, or your team at work. Professionally, having strong social networks and collaborative teams enables you to have greater impact and increase the possibilities available to you. Social networks also give you a support system and a place to exercise influence.

Our connections with others have a significant impact on the quality of our lives. Which relationships matter most to you? You may care deeply about your romantic partner or your children, or you may be single and have a circle of close friends that make up your family. What kind of relationship do you value? How do you measure the quality of those relationships, and how do you invest in them?

Which relationships matter most to you?

Motherhood as Identity

Being a good mother has been highlighted as a major part of female identity. For many women, motherhood indicates success in every area of their lives. Young women often dream of marriage and having children, wondering when and how they will start their families. Ambitious women who have professional aspirations are faced with evaluating what kind of mother they want to be and how they will make the right choices in juggling their different roles. Going from being an individual focusing on yourself and your own ambitions to losing yourself in your children—only to have to find yourself again when your children are grown and on their own—is quite the journey.

How about women who don't have kids, either because they can't for physical reasons or as a personal choice? There is a general assumption that all women want to have children. Choosing otherwise challenges those societal expectations and can bring up feelings of isolation.

How much does your identity as a woman depend on your decisions about motherhood, either being a mother or choosing not to have children? If you are older and entering a new chapter in your life where your kids are grown or more independent, are you happy with your experience mothering them? What did you sacrifice that you can reclaim now?

What does it mean to be successful as a mother? When you think back to your own mother or other women who played a mothering role in your life, how did they affect you or influence your ideas about motherhood?

Social Responsibility

Decades ago, people focused on their local communities and generally lacked the awareness or access to making a greater impact, but times have changed. As women have gained more rights and become more empowered, they have also become more passionate about advocating for others. The ability to contribute to a cause or shed light on an issue that needs to be addressed has become a driving force for many women. Taking social responsibility and advocating for change have become their passion and pursuit.

How do you feel about social responsibility and your contribution to different causes? Are you passionate about the environment, ending poverty, or advocating for women's rights? Maybe you prefer to donate money or volunteer locally. Maybe you don't feel compelled to invest time and energy in any of these areas (which is totally OK).

How do you feel about social responsibility?

When you were growing up, what was the conversation like about volunteering or supporting different causes? How does social responsibility connect to success for you?

Health and Well-Being

You need to have the stamina to keep going until you have completed your tasks. Without health and energy, you can't do anything. When you don't take care of your health, you feel it in all aspects of your life.

Health is a result of prioritizing your physical, emotional, and mental well-being. It took me years to realize the importance of prioritizing my health in order to be present and productive. I know now how important it is to eat the right food, exercise, and get enough sleep. Nor do I underestimate the effect of stress on my ability to focus and on the quality of my relationships.

Often people—especially women who are naturally inclined to be caretakers—take health for granted and don't realize when they have reached burnout. Women especially tend to suffer in silence and often tolerate more distress than they admit. Historically, they were shamed for being too emotional or dramatic, and their physical health was not a primary focus of the male-dominated medical field. To this day, the focus on and investment in women's health and wellness is still behind that of men. Between 2013 and 2023, the amount of funding dedicated to women's health research by the National Institute of Health (NIH) has averaged 8.8 percent.

As a woman, I can't stress enough how important it is to advocate for yourself. You must speak up when it comes to your physical, emotional, and mental well-being. Don't settle for being in pain or feeling depressed or overwhelmed. Seek out resources and make yourself a priority. Don't fall into the trap that many women fall into and take care of everyone around you first. Remember that on an airplane, they always tell you to put on your oxygen mask before helping others. You cannot support the people around you if you don't first make sure that you are healthy, strong, and present.

What do health and well-being look like for you? How do you look and feel? How do you know when you are healthy or experience contentment and peace of mind? What happens when you are stressed out, and how do you decompress?

Personal Growth and Continual Learning

There is something powerful in pushing yourself to grow and learn something new. I'm always signing up for conferences or classes to improve my knowledge or skills about something I need to get better at, or something that frustrates me (like technology). I also listen to audiobooks on subjects from parenting and female health to financial success and leadership skills. I'm a fully committed lifelong learner, and I highly encourage you to become one as well (if you are not already).

I know there are so many options these days that it could feel overwhelming to even to choose something, but start small and give it a try. If you don't get pulled in or feel inspired, choose something else. There is no loss here, only gain.

Personal development is about knowing yourself better so that you can discover strengths and weaknesses in order to pursue your goals, deepen your relationships, and feel more engaged and inspired. When was the last time you learned something new or sought out a way to develop personally? What passion do you have that you could learn more about? How would you know if you were successful in this area?

Personal Fulfillment and Authenticity

Fulfillment and authenticity are part of your personal growth. You may be your own project and believe that the more you pursue your own personal growth, the more authentic you will be. Is that important to you? What was it like being authentic with your family of origin? Could you be completely yourself, or did you adopt attitudes and behaviors that fit in with the group? How does your ability to be truly authentic fit into your definition of success?

How does your ability to be truly authentic fit into your definition of success?

Take Responsibility

As you work to redefine success, the most powerful thing you can do is to take complete responsibility for yourself. You are responsible for making the choices you make, and you are responsible for taking action to achieve your results. When you decide that achieving success in your life is up to you, you stop waiting for external circumstances to help you and you start pursuing opportunities.

Taking responsibility makes you feel in control of your life. When you feel in control, you feel grounded and confident to act.

When I first decided that if I wanted to have, be, and do what I wanted with my life, I realized that it was up to me to make it happen: no one else was going to do it for me. As my dad says, "The distance between dreams and reality is action."

Summary

This chapter stressed the importance of defining success for yourself. We reviewed the three major roles that are available for women today: full-time wife and mother; childless career woman; and a woman who is balancing both roles. The right choice for each woman depends on her idea of her own life and what matters to her.

We also saw how these three roles have evolved since the middle of the last century, so that women have become increasingly integrated into the modern workplace and have been able to increase their status in realms such as business and politics.

The chapter discussed the role of your personal background in determining your attitudes toward life choices. Your family of origins may have imprinted you with messages and beliefs that no longer serve you. The same may be true of the beliefs and expectations of those around you today. You will find it helpful to weed these beliefs out of your mind.

Women of today are seeking achievement and success not just through career advancement, holding leadership roles, or financial independence: there is also great emphasis on going beyond traditional ideas of "work" success. This is closely tied to honoring their authentic selves and pursuing passions that feel meaningful to them—and have an impact on the world at large.

We also considered some of the major pillars of success: professional ambitions, family aspirations, personal fulfillment, and financial security. Health was noted as a major theme, because without solid health, other achievements become difficult if not impossible. We considered the value of lifelong learning. Finally, we stressed the crucial importance of taking responsibility for yourself in all areas.

Step One
Define Success for Yourself in Every Area of Your Life

Action Plan and Exercises

Each of these chapters will end with some exercises to help you reflect on and integrate the ideas presented. Get a journal, or download The Accomplished Woman's Guide at www.theaccomplishedwomanguide.com and find yourself a cozy spot and your favorite pen.

EXERCISE ONE: DEFINE SUCCESS

The first step is to define your idea of success in every area of your life. Go back through each of the areas below. Identify the thoughts and feelings about success that you've internalized and see how they influence your life and choices.

- Career or ambition
- Money
- Health and well-being
- Relationships
- Social responsibility
- Personal growth and well-being
- Family and motherhood

Remember the garden analogy: weed out the ideas and beliefs that no longer serve you. Decide which ideas are true for you now and should remain and which ones no longer serve you and should be let go of.

Then write down your definition of success in each area. What does it look like, and how do you measure it?

EXERCISE TWO:
CREATE YOUR OWN PERSONAL SUCCESS MANIFESTO

Imagine yourself at the end of your life writing to your younger self and reflecting back on all that you have experienced. Go through each of the categories listed above. Tell yourself what you are proud of in each area and how you feel about yourself and the goals you have accomplished.

Really tap into how you feel as you reflect and describe why those achievements matter to you. Feel free to give yourself advice on what choices to make. Remember you are your older self, and you are writing in the present tense about the past. For example: "As I sit here celebrating my eightieth birthday, I reflect back on my life and am so proud of all of my accomplishments . . ."

Now launch yourself into a year from now and reflect on everything you have accomplished over the previous twelve months. Write down what you achieved and how you feel about those achievements.

This is a powerful exercise. When you read it over a year from now, you will be surprised at all that has happened.

Chapter 2
The Power of Clarity and the Process of Setting Goals

PEOPLE ASK ME ALL the time what it was like growing up with the world-renowned author and speaker Brian Tracy as a father. I never know exactly what to say. To many people he has been a mentor, a guide, a voice of possibility, but to me he was just Dad.

When I was around four or five years old, we would walk to a nearby park. He would sit on the swing, I would sit on his lap, and we would swing as high as we could in the hope that he could kick the tall tree that reached out above our heads. I remember believing that if we could just go high enough, we would kick the branch that teased us each time we ascended into the sky. Each time we went up, there was a feeling of excitement and anticipation, not knowing if that would be the time we'd succeed. Each time we fell back, we would laugh off the miss and take a deep breath to reset our commitment. I don't think we ever did touch that branch, but for as long as I can remember, I've always believed in focusing on what you want and working hard to make it happen.

I think that has been the greatest lesson I've taken from having Brian Tracy as a father. He made that me believe anything was possible and that I was capable of achieving anything I could dream of if I was willing to work for it. He talked about having a positive attitude and always expecting the best. If something didn't turn out the way I expected (which happens a lot in your childhood and teen years), he would help me to see the lesson or the opportunity to try something different. He taught me that people who have a plan and go after what they want with a full heart and unwavering belief are the ones who feel the most fulfilled.

As a result, by the time I was in high school, I was a professional planner. I had plans for everything. I had a plan for my career, I had a plan for whom I would marry, and I had a plan for doing well in school and getting into college. My friends would frequently joke with me and ask how my ten-year plan was going (to this day when I see people from my childhood, they often ask how my "plans" have turned out). I was so plan-oriented that on the weekend, I would wake up and start the day off talking with my mom about that day and what our "ideal" plan would be. In fact, I still use my "perfect" day exercise with my family and friends: I ask those around me what would be their perfect day, and once we gather all the ideas, we can see how they fit together into a "perfect" plan so everyone can feel happy with their day.

On Sundays when my dad was in town, we would go to a little place called Le Peep for brunch, just the two of us, and I would catch him up on everything that was going on in my life and he would offer me his fatherly wisdom. One time I remember telling him my plans for my career. He looked up at me and said, "Christina, if you make it a goal and work towards it, then it will happen." Up to that point, I knew that when I made plans to have, be, or do something, I was pretty good at making things happen, but this was the first time I realized that what I had been doing all along was setting goals and creating plans to achieve those goals. I think one of my dad's greatest gifts to me was helping me realize the importance of having and setting goals.

Your Most Valuable Asset

Setting goals is one of the most important things you can do, and nothing is really possible without it. It's about making decisions for what you want to have, be, or do and being proactive with your time and energy in order to realize those hopes and dreams.

Setting goals is one of the most important things you can do.

When you get into the habit of setting goals for yourself and intentionally working towards them, you will find that you are not only more productive with your time, but you will also experience greater satisfaction with your daily accomplishments. Too often people fall into the trap of not setting goals. As a result, they end up reacting to needs of others and find themselves frustrated, guilty, and unfulfilled with how they spent their time.

Time is your most valuable asset, and it is a limited resource. When you take control of how you spend your time, you immediately improve the quality of your life, your ability to attain success, and your personal fulfillment. Setting goals and working towards them is how you take control of your time.

The Importance of Goals

Anybody can achieve goals. You achieve goals all the time—when you decide to get somewhere on time, make dinner, or complete a project. The difference is that those goals are not set with the intention to achieve something greater, that reflects what you are capable of and would have a meaningful impact on your life. Those goals may be things you need to get done, but without bigger, more specific goals, you will find yourself going in circles and feeling unfulfilled.

When you set goals, you unlock your potential to achieve far more than is otherwise possible. Studies show that less than 5 percent of people actually set goals, yet those who do achieve more than anyone else.

Goals provide clarity, focus, and purpose. They make you feel empowered, and they give you direction and objectives to work towards. People always feel happier when they are working toward something that is challenging, exciting, and meaningful to them.

When you align your goals with your personal values and ideals, everything you do becomes more meaningful and rewarding. When your goals and actions are congruent with your priorities, you achieve a greater feeling of balance.

Women especially experience frustration when their lives and their values are not congruent. I can't tell you how many conversations I've had with women who struggle with feeling guilty about how they spend their time. They consistently feel that when you are in one place doing one thing, you feel bad about not being in another place doing a different thing: it seems there is no way to win. This is an ongoing struggle for ambitious women who are still trying to do it all. But when you determine what's important to you, design your life to reflect those values, and choose to spend your time in accordance with them, that alignment gives you a sense of pride and fulfillment, because you know you are investing your time in something that matters.

When we have our values and goals in alignment, we feel great. Anybody who has walked away from a bad situation because it was inconsistent with what they believed to be right gets a tremendous feeling of liberation and relief (not to mention that pit in your stomach also goes away). Even though it may have been a painful choice, making it gives a tremendous boost. At the same time, we've all had the experience of feeling distress when staying in a situation that is inconsistent with our values. Goals guided by your values help you avoid and escape those negative experiences and attract positive, uplifting opportunities.

Four Types of Goals

1. Overarching goals
2. Strategic goals
3. Long-term goals
4. Short-term goals

Four Different Types of Goals
OVERARCHING GOALS

There are four different types of goals. The first is the *overarching goal*, which is based on your fundamental values, beliefs, and desires. It consists of your unifying principles: things that you stand for and that you believe to be valuable and important. You cannot sacrifice these values without feeling bad about yourself.

I believe that one valuable overarching goal is to become everything you are capable of and fulfilling your full potential.

An overarching goal like this becomes a guiding principle, and all other goals should be consistent with it.

Imagine if you were to fulfill your full potential in every area of your life. What would it be like if this was your guiding principle and foundation? In his book *The Road Less Traveled*, M. Scott Peck talks about love and relationships: "Love is the commitment to the full development of the total potential of the other." Love is wanting the other person to fulfill their full potential as a human being. You owe it to yourself to give yourself the same kind of love. Encourage yourself to have, be, and do anything and everything that matters to you.

Love is wanting the other person to fulfill their full potential as a human being.

STRATEGIC GOALS

The second type of goal is *strategic goals*. These are goals that are consistent with and contribute to your overarching goals. If your overarching goal lays your foundation and sets your inner compass, strategic goals guide you to create a life that reflects these values. For example, one of my overarching goals is to experience deep, meaningful relationships and teach others how to do the same. When I set my strategic goals, I always keep in mind how they connect to my mission to live authentically and deeply connected in my relationships. If I set a career goal, I take into account how achieving it would affect my relationships with my husband and children. I start with my foundation and determine my strategic goals from there.

Another way to think about the relation between these two types of goals is that your overarching goal is the *why* behind your *what*. When you set a strategic goal, you are determining *what* you want to achieve; the overarching goal is *why* you want to achieve it. For example, one of my overarching goals is to instill strong family appreciation in my children and husband. To accomplish this, I have set a strategic goal of organizing two family trips a year, which give us time together and solidify family values and connections.

LONG-TERM AND SHORT-TERM GOALS

The best thing to do when setting goals is to set both long-term and short-term goals. You can start with setting goals for five years into the future by asking yourself where you would like to be in every area of your life at that point.

Having clarified that, you can work backwards and break your goals down into smaller amounts of time. You can break down a five-year goal into years, months, and even weekly benchmarks and check-ins that ensure you keep taking steps toward the accomplishment of each goal. If five years seem too far into the future, start with setting goals for the next year and set monthly benchmarks so you keep the momentum and experience the reward much sooner. Once you see that it works, you will feel inspired to set longer-term goals with more opportunities for motivating and rewarding yourself.

At the beginning of January, I sit down and review my goals from the previous year and then set goals for the new year. I keep in mind my five-year goals, but take it a year at a time. I find that coming up with monthly benchmarks keeps me motivated and on track. My husband and I started doing this with our kids several years ago. When we review their goals, they're always surprised to find how many things on their lists they've achieved.

In fact, here is a simple exercise: write down a list of five to ten things you want to achieve, put it in an envelope, and put it away. Open it up twelve months from now, and you will be astonished to find that about 80 percent of your list will have been accomplished over the year, even though you never opened the envelope once.

Write down a list of five to ten things you want to achieve, put it in an envelope, and put it away for a year.

The Goal Setting Process

How exactly do you go about setting goals? Where do you start? The concept can seem overwhelming, and sometimes people have a hard time starting. But goal setting is fun: it's about getting to decide what you want (almost like writing a wish list for the holidays). Here is a four-step process to get you started.

Goal setting is fun: it's about getting to decide what you want.

Step One: Evaluate Your Situation

When working with goals, we start by evaluating our current situation. Most people don't do this, because it can be emotionally hard to become aware of what might not be working for you or bringing you joy. To take responsibility for your life requires a lot of effort and commitment. Deciding to start or stop a behavior can create anxiety for people who enjoy the security of what they know versus fearing the risks of what they don't know. But in order to feel empowered, you have to be conscious of the choices you are making and determine the changes you want to make and the dreams you want to work towards.

Ask yourself what exactly is going on in your life right now. Are you happy with your job, relationships, and physical health? Be painfully honest with yourself and give yourself permission to not be perfect. Brutal honesty is the beginning of the path to success and fulfillment.

Next, write out a clear definition of your desired future reality. How do you want your future to be? What do you want it to look like? Imagine you have a magic wand that you can wave to create anything you want. There is no limitation on time, money, skill, or opportunity. Just let yourself fantasize about your ideal situation. It's amazing how much we automatically limit ourselves (too expensive, not enough time, people won't support it, it's not justified) when we try to imagine our perfect reality. Just let your mind create whatever it can come up with. Include every aspect of your life as you would have it be.

Now compare your current reality to your description of your ideal future. You can create a side-by-side chart that describes your current situation on one side and your ideal future on the other side. Then you can list the differences between the two. Ask yourself what you are going to have to do to get from where you are to where you want to be. That is the starting point of fulfilling your potential, achieving success, and living life on your own terms—

the starting point of an exhilarating feeling of high self-esteem, control, advancement, and growth. This is the beginning of the empowered and creative process which moves you from where you are to where you want to be. Think about it: you wouldn't put in your destination address without also entering a starting point.

Step Two: Write Down Your Goals

Now that you've envisioned your ideal future, it's time to identify and write down the goals that will turn that vision into a reality. Write down goals for each area of your life. There are several categories of goals. Here are some examples:

Spiritual goals relate to peace of mind, tranquility, and harmony. They can also include your religious path and anything else that qualifies as spiritual to you.

Family and relationship goals relate to your home, children, and romantic connections. How do you want your homelife to be, what do you want for your children, and what is important in order for you to have a loving relationship with your partner? (Personally, I break this out into two sections, with both a "family" category and "relationship" category, because they are both very significant areas for defining success for myself.)

This category typically has a strong influence on why you are doing what you are doing in other areas of your life. It also has a strong impact on your feeling of balance when you are not congruent.

Social goals are connected to your friendships and social life. How much do you value your peer group? What kind of dynamic do you want to have? Some people prefer to invest in a small number of friends and enjoy intimate interactions over coffee or a meal;

others want a robust social life, hosting gatherings and bringing people together. What friendships are important to you, and how do you stay connected?

Health and fitness goals. What kind of energy and vitality do you want to have? How do you want to feel in your body? What physical goals do you have for yourself? This also relates to your health and longevity—what will you do to ensure a quality life.

Career, ambition, and financial goals. If you are pursuing a career, what do you hope to achieve? How much money do you want to make? How will you apply your skills? How will you determine if you are excelling in your role? Later we will talk about turning your natural talents into tangible assets or even creating your own business. Make sure to include financial goals for earning, saving, and spending.

Material goals focus on home, car, clothes, and other tangible goods. If you want a new home or a new car, write down a specific, detailed description of exactly what you want, such as layout, location, and yard, or color, make, and model. (This is my husband's least favorite category, because it's all about spending money, so he's always happy when my list here is short).

Personal development. This is where you would explore what kind of person you want to be. What qualities do you want to develop? Do you want to be a good public speaker, writer, or artist? Do you want to be more courageous, self-confident, or outspoken? Maybe you strive to be a calmer, more relaxed, and more mindful person. Do you want to develop some hobby or skill that inspires you? Your personal development is really the basis of your success in any area, because to know yourself and develop your strengths while accepting your weaknesses is the way you live authentically and experience more self-fulfillment.

Community service goals. How do you want to serve the people in your community? What charities do you want to support? What causes do you desire to advocate for? Your support and social network play a major role in your impact, so investing in your community gives you the ability to make a bigger difference. How would you like to invest your time and energy in this area?

Your goals must be clearly defined, measurable, realistic, in your control, and attainable. Goals need to be measurable and concrete so that you can keep track of your progress. Create mental pictures of your goals by turning a concept like financial success, optimal health, or happiness into an action or state you can see yourself in or doing. What amount of money is financial success? You need a number. Optimal health means what to you? Does it mean running five miles three times a week, or sleeping eight solid hours every night?

Happiness to me means spending an hour every morning reading and drinking coffee while everyone else sleeps. What does it look like for you?

Realistic means that if you wanted to make more money, you would not set a goal to increase your income by 1000 percent over the next two years, although it would be realistic to increase your annual income by 50 percent. If your goal is not realistic and achievable, you will find yourself struggling to start working towards it, because on some level, you know you will fail.

In your control means you can only set goals for yourself You can't set goals for other people, for example, you can't set a goal that your partner will take up exercising and lose twenty pounds. However, if you are in a relationship and as a couple choose to set goals together for the relationship, family, or anything else that feels like a collaboration (which I highly recommend), that is a different scenario: here you have mutual buy-in.

You write down your goal in the present tense, as though it is already a reality. For example, you might say something like "I complete my book by the September deadline," or "I weigh 130 pounds and experience consistent energy throughout the day." You begin to manifest your own reality; you can even use images and visualization to see yourself having accomplished the goal.

Many people swear by the power of creating a vision board, which is a visual representation of each of your written goals. The best technique for creating a vision board is to first write down your goals, then to gather images that show each goal achieved, placing them on a board that you consistently see. Each time you look at your board, you activate your mental pictures and are reminded of the goals you have set for yourself.

Many people swear by the power of creating a vision board.

Written (especially handwritten) goals signal commitment and give you a means of accountability. You can only review your goals and keep track of your progress when they are documented. You must write them down, because according to Brian, in his book *Goals*, "A goal that is not written is not a goal at all. It is merely a wish, a dream, or a fantasy."

Writing down a goal programs it into your subconscious mind. When you write it in the present tense, as though it is already a reality, you begin to enforce a self-fulfilling prophecy. It takes on a force and power all of its own, and amazing things will happen. We believe what we are told. If we declare that something is a reality for ourselves in the form of a goal, we begin to believe that it is our reality. Once we believe it, we can achieve it.

Now with your goals set, let's prioritize them so you can stay focused on what matters most.

Step Three: Prioritize Your Goals

You've made a list of everything you want to accomplish in the next one to five years in the categories of personal development, family, social life, spiritual, financial, relationship, work, and career Now it's time to organize and prioritize your list of goals.

The first step is assigning to each goal an A, B, or a C. *A goals* are those that are really important to you, that you would really love to accomplish. *B goals* are ones that would be nice to accomplish, but they're not as important as the A goals. *C goals* are low priority. It would be nice if they happened, but there is no urgency.

On your list you may have three, four, or five A goals. Prioritize them as A1, A2, A3, and so on. Your A1 is the most important goal of all and becomes your major definite purpose in that category. Ask yourself, "If I could only accomplish one thing on this list, which would be the most valuable and important to me?" I also like to think of this question as it relates specifically to each category. For example, "Which goal would have the greatest impact on my career or financial success?" or "Which goal would have most significant impact on my family?"

Then ask, "If there was just one more thing I could achieve, which item on this list would be the next most important to me?" That will be your A2. Then define your A3, and so on.

Now that you've prioritized your goals, let's explore why those goals truly matter to you.

Step Four: Identify the "Why"

For your most important goals (A1–A5), determine why you want to achieve each one. How will achieving it affect your life? Here you identify the "why" behind your goal: as I've already pointed out, your "why" fuels your momentum and commitment. You need to know the reason for and benefit from accomplishing each goal.

For some people, it is also helpful to identify the cost or consequence of *not* achieving the goal. It depends on whether you're a carrot or stick kind of person. Personally, I use the benefit or reward to determine the reason for my goals, and I reflect on the consequence of not achieving them as a way to stay motivated and focused.

Four Steps in Goal Setting

1. Evaluate your current situation and determine the ideal vision of your future.
2. Break your vision down into categories, and write down your goals for each one.
3. Prioritize your goals.
4. Identify the "why" behind the goal.

Goal Achievement Strategies
SET A DEADLINE

Set a deadline and create a schedule for accomplishment. It's very important to set a deadline for each goal, for several reasons. Once you have a deadline, you can work backwards and create a schedule of benchmarks to keep yourself focused and motivated. Having a deadline also creates accountability with yourself and creates an intensity that feeds into your momentum. If you do not set a deadline, your goal is merely a wish, a hope, or a dream: something nice that might happen one day.

Your goal needs to have a plan of action, a schedule for progress, and a deadline for achievement. The deadline you set will be based on the goal itself and how long you will realistically need to achieve it. Easier, smaller goals will warrant shorter deadlines, whereas big, lofty goals will need more time: deadlines that are six months to a year (if not more) in the future.

You may set a deadline and work towards it, but circumstances may come up that may require you to reevaluate it. As Brian says, "Be clear about your goal but flexible about the process of achieving it . . . a lot of unexpected and unpredictable events will occur to help move you toward your goal." These events have their own timeline. You need to be open to adapting to new information and circumstances.

MAKE A LIST

Name each goal and list out everything you can think of that is necessary to achieve each one. What are all the steps you imagine you would need to take to get from where you are to where you want to be?

BREAK GOALS INTO MANAGEABLE STEPS

Once you have your deadline and list, you can use the list to break your goal down into smaller steps and set a deadline for each task. You could have a daily task or a weekly task.

It is much easier for most people to break a large project or goal into easier, smaller steps, because then they feel each step is easily achievable. When you complete each one, you will experience a boost of enthusiasm that propels you toward the next task. If I write a list of things I need to do at the beginning of the day and I'm able to check off all the items at the end of the day, I feel great; I feel I've had a very satisfying, productive day. Science tells us that accomplishing a task activates the reward center of the brain, so this feeling of satisfaction is the result of brain chemistry.

It's amazing: every step that you take toward the accomplishment of a goal that is important to you will give you a feeling of well-being, energy, enthusiasm, and self-esteem. By contrast, every day that passes in which you *don't* move toward an important goal will give you a feeling of fatigue, dissatisfaction, and going around in circles.

IDENTIFY OBSTACLES

Obstacles, which come in many forms, can easily distract or prevent us from moving towards our goals. Sometimes I've set aside time to work on a project, but it's been sidetracked when I get a call from the school telling me I have to pick up my sick child. I've hit an obstacle when I expected certain money to be available, but it wasn't. I had to change my timeline and adapt to the financial obstacle. Like many people, I had big plans for the year 2020, but the Covid pandemic was a huge obstacle to progress and a real test of determination.

Determine the obstacles that may confront you: what would prevent you from achieving your goals. Your obstacles could be time or money, but they could also be people or circumstances you will need to navigate. Kids create an unpredictability factor on a daily basis. Anticipate how you will deal with problems like a sick child so that it does not deter you from achieving your goals.

Identify as many obstacles as you can so you can determine how to overcome each one. Sometimes the obstacle is within, telling you that you can't achieve your goal or you are not good enough. These obstacles are just as distracting as external ones.

Once you've determined everything you must overcome as thoroughly as possible, focus on removing the biggest obstacle. There is usually one "big rock" in the way: if you remove all the little rocks (smaller, less difficult barriers) first, you will still be blocked by this big rock. It is your number one obstacle. In fact, it usually makes up 80 percent of the impediments between you and your goal. When you remove it, it will do more to move you toward your goal than everything else put together.

This big rock may be a relationship. It may be your health or your level of education. It may be a coworker, your boss, or your company. Sometimes our biggest obstacles are the things we feel the most distressed by or most reluctant to change, but when you stop or let go of something that isn't working anymore, you make room for something new.

ACQUIRE THE NECESSARY KNOWLEDGE

Determine what knowledge or skill you may need to acquire to achieve your goal.

Everything is learnable. Once you determine that you need to learn something in order to take the next step towards your goal, you can access the necessary information anywhere. You can take an online course, read a book, watch a video on YouTube, or even reach out to an expert in the field and ask for advice or mentorship.

People often underestimate themselves, thinking they are not capable of achieving what others have achieved, but the truth is, you can learn anything and develop any skill you desire. You just have to commit to the process and use your self-discipline to develop the skill and apply it.

Nevertheless, you may have a natural talent in one area but really struggle in another. It might not make sense for you to learn a new skill and work on your weakness. It might make more sense to collaborate with someone, hire someone, or form a partnership with another person who excels in the area you do not. For example, I'm not particularly good with technology, and social media often baffles me. I've tried to learn how to do it myself, but it takes me so much time that I decided it was more valuable to focus on areas where I can develop more easily and recruit someone to help me with building my own website and managing my social media platforms.

Can you think of a type of knowledge or a skill that would help you achieve one of your goals?

IDENTIFY HELPERS

No one achieves success alone. We need people to support, encourage, and guide us along the way. They could include people who support you and take on responsibilities so you have more time, or they may provide you with needed opportunities.

Identify the people in your life who will help you achieve your goals. They may be individuals you already know, but they might also be people you need to introduce yourself to or ask to be connected with.

More and more, I have come to appreciate the importance of community and social support, especially for women. Whether it's asking for help or discovering ways to collaborate, connecting with other people not only supports your quest, but makes it feel like you have your own team.

VISUALIZE YOUR ACHIEVEMENTS

Visualization is a powerful tool to move you toward your goal. Create mental pictures of yourself once you've achieved your goal; imagine yourself having, being, and doing exactly what you want. Then connect to how you will feel emotionally after having achieved the goal. It's amazing how visualizing an ideal outcome will affect your expectations and inspire you to feel enthusiastic, positive, and confident to take even more action.

UTILIZE THE LAW OF RESONANCE

Everything is energy. Your outer world reflects your inner world, so your thoughts become things. The pictures you hold in your mind have a certain frequency of energy. When you set a goal, you are creating a mental picture of something you want that has its own frequency. Through the law of resonance, you will activate this frequency and draw what you want to you.

Unfortunately, this works for both positive and negative mental pictures, so you always want to think about what you want instead of what you don't want.

Here is an example of the law of resonance: when you have two pianos in the same room, if you hit a key on one piano, you will find that that same key is vibrating on the other.

You can experiment with this law by choosing to think about something you really want. Then pay attention to how often you see a reflection of that thing around you.

This is why it is especially important to create clear, measurable, written goals: so you can see mental pictures of what you want and put out a clear frequency that draws opportunities to you. Your goals will allow you to focus on an outcome and activate the law of attraction.

CELEBRATE THE WINS

Keep up your momentum and motivation by celebrating the wins along the way. Acknowledge each task completion in some way, and celebrate the wins. Some people are really good at delayed gratification, but most people need more regular feedback. If you find a way to reward yourself for hitting the checkpoints or benchmarks, you will boost your motivation for the next task.

Once I set a goal of losing twenty pounds. Since that seemed like such daunting task, I decided to break it up into five-pound checkpoints. I bought myself four gift cards to my favorite stores and vowed not to buy anything unless I used a gift card. Each time I lost five pounds, I rewarded myself with a gift card and got to buy myself something new. It was a lot of work to achieve that goal, but being able to celebrate along the way helped with the momentum and made it much more fun.

Summary

Hopefully by now you are convinced of the value and importance of setting goals. Remember, you want to be in control of your time, and you only want to spend time on the things that matter most to you and truly reflect your values. If you aren't working to achieve your own goals, you will end up working to achieve the goals of others.

Determine what you really want to achieve in every area of your life. Then use the guidelines in this chapter to set goals that will empower you to experience a life that feels successful and fulfilling on your own terms.

Step Two
Determine what you want to Have, Be, or Do and Set Goals for Every Area of Your Life

Action Plan and Exercises
It's time to grab your journal or download The Accomplished Woman's guide, grab your pen, and find a cozy spot.

EXERCISE ONE: GOAL SETTING WORKSHEET
The purpose of this exercise is to give you a guide to make it easy for you to go through the steps of the goal setting process and identify the strategies that will support you to achieve any goal you set for yourself.

Step One: Where Are You Now?
Reflect on your starting point. What's going well? What needs work in these areas?

Career	Finances
Health	Personal development
Relationships	Community and social life

Step Two: What Do You Want?
Imagine your ideal life. If you could have anything you want, what do you really want in these areas?

Career	Finances
Health	Personal development
Relationships	Community and social life

Step 3: Set Goals.

Write one clear and specific goal for each category. Write a positive statement in the present tense, like "I have..." "I am..." "I earn..."

Step 4: Why Do These Goals Matter?

Why is each goal important to you? How will achieving the goal affect your life? Write down an answer for each goal:

1.
2.
3.
4.
5.
6.

Step Six: Set deadlines.

Pick a deadline for each goal:

Goal 1.
Goal 2.
Goal 3.
Goal 4.
Goal 5.
Goal 6.

Step Seven: Break Down Your Goals

Take each goal and break it down into three small steps. Give each step its own deadline.

Step 8: Stay on Track

For each goal, identify the following:
- What could get in your way?
- Who can help you?
- What knowledge or skill do you need to achieve your goal?
- How will you celebrate small wins?

EXERCISE TWO: CREATE A VISION BOARD

The purpose of this exercise is to create a visual representation of each goal you have set for yourself.

1. You will need a large piece of paper or cardboard, scissors, tape or glue, a magazine or printed out images, and any visual symbols you would like to include.
2. Go through each goal and determine what it will look like when you achieve that goal. Find or create an image that represents that and put it on the board.
3. Write the actual goal on a small notecard or sticky note and place it near the corresponding image.
4. When you are finished, place your vision board in a location that you see daily. This will remind you of what you are working towards, it will activate the law of attraction, and it will help you focus on what matters to you.

Chapter 3
Build Your Confidence, Overcome Self-Doubt, and Cultivate Resilience

Courage is not the absence of fear, but the triumph over it. The brave man is not he who does not feel afraid, but he who conquers that fear.
—NELSON MANDELA

FEELING FEAR IS A part of life. In order to grow, you have to get through the fear to the other side. One of my greatest fears has been public speaking, yet from the time I was a young child I have felt compelled to speak up and advocate for what I believe is important. Over and over again I have felt paralyzed by fear, but at the same time, I have conjured up the courage to act in spite of the fear.

I remember the first time I spoke in public. I was seven years old and was attending a local Montessori school. The school had been using temporary buildings to teach the students, and they finally decided to apply for a permit to build a permanent structure. Unfortunately, several of the local neighbors did not like this idea, and as a result, the issue had to be debated at a city hall meeting. The heads of the school needed the support of the community, and I wanted to help. I went to my dad and told him that I wanted to assist the school in getting their permanent structure. I asked him what I could do. He told me it would be a good idea if I could speak up at the city hall meeting.

My stomach dropped at the thought of speaking in front of a group of people. "Dad", I said, "I can't do that. I'm seven years old."

He turned to me and said, "Christina, if you want to speak up for your school, I will help you write a speech. You can practice and give it at the city hall meeting." He said this in a matter-of-fact way and with much conviction.

I was really nervous about the idea, but since he seemed so confident that I would do a great job, I decided to trust him and give it a try. I really cared about my school and felt that it deserved a real building.

We worked on the speech together, and I practiced it over and over again until I had it memorized. I practiced it in front of the mirror. I practiced with my mother, and I practiced with my little brother, Michael. I just kept practicing.

However, when the time finally came, I still felt scared. Those darn butterflies would not leave my stomach, no matter how much I practiced and how much I told myself it would be OK. There was no turning back: the clock just kept moving toward the time of the meeting, and we had to go.

I was sitting with my mom and dad towards the back of the room. I watched as a panel of adults in front of me discussed and heard people as they came up one by one to plead their case. Then it was my turn. I walked up to the podium with my little speech in hand (just in case). As I got closer, I realized I was too short to see over the top. I looked to my side, saw an empty chair, and pulled it over behind the podium. I took a big step up and stood there looking at the panel, as tall as any adult. I took a deep breath and gave my talk. As far as I remember, it was well received, and ultimately the school got their permit to build.

My first talk had been a success, but my fear of public speaking did not go away. I've spent decades learning from my father (a world-renowned public speaker), teaching with my father (yes, I specialize in teaching people public speaking and presenting skills), and speaking all over the world to groups big and small. Still, every time I speak to an audience, I feel the butterflies. Each time I'm provided with an opportunity to call on my courage to get me through the fear.

As a seven-year-old, I needed my dad to believe in me, so I'd take the chance. Now that I'm an adult, I realize how important it is for me to believe in myself. That belief convinces me to try, and each time I try, I feel a little more confident that I can do it. The more confident I am, the more I do, and the more courage I have to keep doing it.

Take Action

Now that you've defined what success looks like for you, determined exactly what you want to have, be, or do in each area of your life and documented what you want with written goals, the next big step is to take action. This is where self-confidence, your ability to overcome self-doubt, and your resilience for navigating life's challenges determines how you move forward.

Self-Confidence versus Self-Doubt

Self-confidence is the inner fuel behind your ability to act. When you have self-confidence and believe in yourself and what you can achieve, you are more willing to act, try new things, and take initiative towards opportunities. The belief in yourself is the key to unlocking your potential and the accelerator to achieving your goals.

Self-confidence is the inner fuel behind your ability to act.

The biggest obstacle to building your self-confidence is self-doubt. Everyone experiences self-doubt at some point: even the most successful, capable people you know have moments of doubt. Self-doubt serves a purpose: it keeps us safe. Maybe you are familiar with the comfort zone: it's the place of what we know and what feels comfortable; it's also the place where self-doubt flourishes. When we experience self-doubt, we tend to hesitate and procrastinate when it comes to taking action. We then fall into a cycle of questioning our abilities and worthiness, ultimately delaying our achievements.

Part of our journey in this life is to acknowledge which thoughts and behaviors keep us safe and stuck in our comfort zone (we aren't good enough, we need more training, we don't have value to offer, someone else can do it better, etc.). Then we can discover the steps we need to take in order to grow and move beyond our comfort zone and experience greater joy, confidence, and fulfillment. Getting yourself out of your comfort zone is how you start to cultivate resilience.

Life is full of unexpected twists and turns. Your ability to be flexible and bounce back from failures and setbacks determines how you feel about life. When you cultivate resilience, you boost your self-confidence and have greater trust in the unknown. For many people, unexpected setbacks trigger a feeling of being out of control, and when you feel out of control, it causes anxiety and worry.

But when you develop resilience and learn to trust that you can bounce back, you become able to tolerate situations when things feel out of control. You learn that things might not work out, but you realize that no matter what happens, you will be OK. Believing this fact will boost your self-confidence. It will also encourage you to try new things, and it will support you when you fall back into your comfort zone.

In this chapter, we are going to explore how to build your self-confidence so you feel empowered to take risks, seize opportunities, and feel a greater sense of control. We will explore the nature of the comfort zone, how it serves us, and how we can escape it in order to overcome self-doubt. You will learn techniques to help you cultivate resilience and bounce back from any situation. Ultimately, you are going to learn three essential ideas that will propel you from thinking about what you want to actually going after it.

You Can Get the Job Done

Confidence is the trust and belief in ourselves that we can learn and adapt to meet our needs and achieve the goals we set for ourselves. Confidence also fuels our enthusiasm for action. If we believe we are capable of making something happen, we are more likely to try. If we lack confidence and don't think we can do something, we will hesitate to act or will find excuses to procrastinate.

Confidence fuels our enthusiasm for action.

I find that confidence is also connected to being clear. I know that if I find myself stuck or not taking action, most of the time it's because I'm not clear, or I don't know how to do what I'm expected to do. Being unclear about what you need to do (or are being asked to do) triggers self-doubt, but if you ask for clarification on the task and understand the results you are aiming for, you immediately feel more confident about taking action.

This idea will come up again in other chapters, but in the case of confidence, the more you know which steps to take and the more competent you believe you are in taking them, the more confidence and enthusiasm you will have to take them.

Confidence is knowing you can get the job done. It is knowing that you can live up to the needs and expectations of yourself and the people around you. Without that self-confidence, you might struggle to move forward, never try new things, and end up feeling stuck and going in circles. The good thing is that anyone can build up their self-confidence; it's a learnable trait.

Self-Confidence and Self-Esteem

Self-confidence is believing in yourself and your abilities, whereas self-esteem is more about your self-worth and how you value yourself. Your self-esteem refers more to who you are and how much you respect yourself regardless of your achievements; it is knowing you have value just for being you. Self-confidence is much more connected to what you can do, and it can be influenced by success or failure. The two are related in that if you have high self-esteem, you tend to have more self-confidence. When you believe in your value, you are more likely to take on challenges confidently, with a positive, optimistic attitude. Every time you accomplish a task or get positive feedback, it boosts your self-esteem.

My dad has always taught me that high self-esteem and self-confidence are the result of three things:

1. **A feeling of mastery, competence, and control.** Nothing will make you feel better about yourself and more in control of your life than knowing you are good at what you do. On the other hand, nothing will diminish your self-esteem more than knowing you are only average or poor at what you do. That's why, whenever you get a compliment or recognition for having done a good job, you feel great about yourself. The opposite is true if you get negative feedback.
2. **A sense of personal growth and fulfillment.** Several studies show that when we are growing and working towards an objective, we feel good about ourselves. As soon as we stop growing and learning, we start to feel negative, apathetic, and bored. This affects every area of our lives.
3. **A history of achievement and success.** If you've had success in the past, you will have greater self-confidence and are more likely to look for success in the present.

The Foundation of Self-Confidence is built from:
1. A feeling of mastery, competence, and control
2. A sense of personal growth and fulfillment
3. A history of achievement and success

How Do You Build Self-Confidence?

In my work with people—whether it's coaching them to become professional speakers or working with them as a therapist to overcome psychological obstacles and insecurities—I find that in order to build self-confidence, you have to start with self-worth or self-esteem. Acceptance is really the foundation of self-worth, yet most people struggle to accept themselves for who they are.

Often people come to me to help them overcome a part of themselves that they've decided doesn't fit in with everyone else. It's heartbreaking to watch people devalue themselves because they are comparing themselves to others instead of trusting in their own value. No one is perfect, I believe; everyone has their quirks. We all have insecurities, odd habits, and particular needs or preferences. That's what makes each person special and unique. If we try to eliminate what makes us different, we limit our ability to offer our own unique gifts in our work and our relationships.

Self-acceptance is about liking yourself. You have to accept and like yourself before you will trust that others will like and accept you. My dad tells people to stand in front of a mirror and say out loud, "I like myself; I like myself; I like myself." It makes me cringe just writing this down, because I always felt that that was so cheesy. Personally, I struggled because it didn't feel authentic to just declare that I liked myself. I couldn't say something unless I believed it, and in order to really believe it, I needed more. If I was going to say, "I like myself," I wanted to know *why* I liked myself. What about me was I proud of or believed to be a likable characteristic? Some people can say something and accept it; others, like me, need a reason or evidence to believe it's true.

If you can look in the mirror, say, "I like myself," and feel good about it, I encourage you to try the exercise above. If you need more before you can do that, make a list of all the things you like about yourself. What makes you valuable? Sometimes people struggle with this, so I suggest that you imagine someone is interviewing your closest friend or partner. What would they say makes you a likable person? This may sound silly, but I promise if you do it, you will shift your inner dialogue, and amazing things will happen. Try it: take a moment right now and think about something you like about yourself or something about you that you are proud of. Try not to smile.

Make a list of all the things you like about yourself.

As I've mentioned earlier, self-esteem is about who you are and how you perceive yourself, whereas confidence is about what you can do. It comes from believing in your ability to perform tasks, handle situations, and get results.

How do you build a belief that you are able to do things and do them well? You have to prove to yourself that you can do them well. The greatest factor in building confidence is developing competency. I have found both personally and professionally that nothing makes you feel better about yourself than knowing you are good at something.

How do you get good at something? You learn how to do it. If you want to be more technologically savvy, you need to practice using computers. If you want to have better relationships, you need to practice using communication skills (among many other things). If you want to be a long-distance runner, you need to start jogging short distances to build up your stamina.

Whenever you try something new and get a good result, it makes you feel more competent. If you know that you can succeed, you will have positive expectations (because you know you will get a good result). The positive expectations fuel your confidence and generate enthusiasm. As a result, you are more passionate and excited to act. Then the cycle repeats. Each time you have a success, you gain a win and a mental picture of your positive results. Having a win that you can refer to fortifies your belief in your competency, and each time you remind yourself of that success, you get a boost of confidence. Once you've had that one great success, your subconscious drives you to repeat it. It is a model or mental picture you can use to boost your confidence and drive you towards more success. Can you think of a recent win or success in your life? How did it make you feel to experience it?

Visualization and Affirmation

Another powerful technique to boost your confidence is to visualize yourself succeeding. It's amazing what impact it has on your whole experience when you start at the end and decide that it's going to be a great success and that you'll feel happy and satisfied.

Visualize yourself succeeding.

Here is an example: Let's say you are going to give a presentation at work. You imagine yourself at the end of the presentation proudly looking at your colleagues as they smile at you with great appreciation. You imagine feeling very proud of yourself and happy with your effort. Once you do this, every time you think about the presentation, you will feel optimistic and positive about the outcome, so you are happy and confident. These positive feelings inspire enthusiasm and high energy, which you then use to deliver your powerful presentation. Throughout this process, you use affirmations to tell yourself that you will be delivering great value in an enjoyable way and that your colleagues will be thankful.

Here is another example: Let's say you've been invited to a party, and you feel anxious about interacting in larger groups. You would imagine yourself at the party feeling relaxed and having comfortable conversations with a couple of people. You see yourself smiling and having a good time. You imagine other people engaging in conversations with you and you feeling connected and accepted by the group. Now, as you get ready for this party, you will be anticipating a comfortable, positive experience, which will help you feel more relaxed and excited. As a result, when you get to the party, you will be smiling and friendly. This will draw people to your positive energy, and you will end up having a great time.

Stuck in the Comfort Zone

What is the comfort zone?

The greatest enemy of action is the comfort zone: it is your biggest obstacle to getting what you want. We all have one: it's a mental space where we feel safe, comfortable, and in complete control. In the comfort zone, tasks are familiar and easy. Everything is predictable, and there are no risks.

The problem is that in order to take action, grow your abilities, and develop self-confidence, you need to leave the comfort zone. This is uncomfortable and can be very distressing. Most people would rather avoid this discomfort and just stay in the cozy comfort zone. But as you let opportunities pass you by, over time you become less engaged in life, and it becomes monotonous. You might even feel discouraged and stuck.

Nothing grows in the comfort zone. Novelty and growth are what inject us with vitality, curiosity, and greater passion. We need new energy to stay vibrant, and new energy only exists beyond the comfort zone.

Paralyzed by Fear

People stay in the comfort zone because they fear failure and judgment from others. It's hard to make a change from something you know to something you don't know.

The fear of failure is one of the most powerful fears. It can be paralyzing, and for some people it takes over as soon as they think about trying something different or taking a risk. They will stay in unsatisfying jobs rather than pursuing their dreams of, say, starting their own business, because they are afraid it will fail. People will stay in terrible relationships because they are afraid to leave and be alone. They fear that they will never find another partner.

The fear of failure is one of the most powerful fears.

At the root of this fear is judgment and the fear of rejection. If you fail, whom will you disappoint? What will other people think if you decide to do something and it doesn't work out? We are social creatures, and a sense of belonging and acceptance from others powerfully influences our behavior. We'd rather sacrifice a desire for something more and remain the same in order to preserve our status in a relationship. Many people have grown up with conditional love: on a deep level they believe that if they fail at something, not only will they have to deal with the disappointment, but they will risk having love withheld by someone important to them.

I've worked with many clients who were never encouraged to make their own choices and try new things. Instead, they were told what to do or encouraged to make particular choices that their parents believed were the "right" ones. These people grew up not just fearing failure but not even knowing how to choose for themselves or have an opinion about something. They are afraid that their choice will be wrong, and they will experience rejection.

Leaving the comfort zone and doing something new and different is especially challenging if your actions will have an impact on people around you. Just as you may feel comfortable in the known and predictable, so do they. If you make a change, it will force them to adjust, ultimately pushing them out of their comfort zone.

People frequently feel that it is very much in their best interest to keep you to stay in your comfort zone. I see this all the time with couples: if one partner makes a big change that will strongly impact the other, that partner tends to protest. However, if you tell your partner what you are thinking of doing and ask for their support, the transition tends to be smoother. You can also ask how you can make this change in a way that considers your partner and helps them to adjust with you. This approach can work in all different kinds of relationship dynamics, not just romantic partnerships. But it starts with you wanting to make a change and being willing to leave your comfort zone.

You know you are stuck in the comfort zone when you find yourself avoiding new challenges or no longer being curious about new opportunities. You may feel unmotivated during the day and not fully engaged in what you are doing. Tasks that are familiar are easy, but we crave challenges. We are most engaged with tasks that present some challenge.

Think about driving. When you drive the same route to work or school, you barely pay attention to the drive or the landmarks along the way. However, if you have to take a new route, you stay alert, pay attention to details, and notice far more.

The same is true for life: you can either choose the comfort zone and live on cruise control, getting to the same place the same way every day, or you can choose a new route, where you discover new experiences and growth opportunities.

The Self-Doubt Monster

Self-doubt is that negative voice in your head that tells you you are not good enough, smart enough, or capable enough. It's the voice that tries to convince you that you can't do what you want because you are lacking in some way. It might even tell you that if you try something new, you will fail and face consequences.

Self-doubt is caused by many things, including childhood experiences, fear of failure (as mentioned above), social pressure,

Build Your Confidence, Overcome Self-Doubt, and Cultivate Resilience

and the constant comparison to others. I like to think of it as a monster that was created out of someone else's fear and has grown over your life. Whenever something didn't work out or someone else told you that you weren't good enough, that self-doubt monster was fed and got stronger and stronger. The more we feed it with our thoughts and negative self-talk, the more powerful it becomes.

The good news is that you can defeat the self-doubt monster. You can liberate yourself from being held back and become all that you were meant to be. You do this by paying attention to your inner dialogue and reframing any critical thoughts about yourself into more encouraging ones. Stop thinking, "I can't . . ." and start thinking, "I'm learning to, and eventually I will be able to . . ."

Stop thinking, "I can't . . ." and start thinking, "I'm learning to, and eventually I will be able to . . ."

We've already seen how you learn to do things through effort and practice. Here your goal is to embrace learning and adopt a growth mindset. A growth mindset is based on progress over perfection. It helps you shift your own self-judgment from "I can't" to "I can" and gives you permission to try something new, whether it works the first time or not. With a growth mindset, you trust that when something doesn't work out, it is a learning experience and an opportunity to pivot and try it a different way. Anyone who has had great success will tell you that they had to fail their way to success. Things not working out is just part of the process. The more you are willing to fail, the more likely you are to succeed.

The Inner Cheerleader

Another approach I like to teach is the idea of recruiting your own inner cheerleader. It's like a best friend that lives in your mind. Whenever you need support or encouragement, your inner cheerleader is the voice that pumps you up and tells you that you can do it! She represents someone who believes in you. She is there with you even when you are scared to move forward. The more conversations you have with her, the more courage you have and the more willing you are to move forward and act.

Think about your own inner cheerleader (I promise you have one). What does she say that gives you a boost of confidence when you are unsure? Mine usually says, "I know you're scared, but you can do this!"

You have to act despite your fear. It's the only way to fulfill your dreams and achieve your goals. Fear lives at the edge of your comfort zone. As soon as you get close to that edge, you start to feel anxious, your heart rate increases, and your palms sweat. It's your mind's way of protecting you from the unknown and keeping you safe.

Here is how you outsmart fear: you tell yourself that you are not afraid; there is nothing unsafe, only unknown. Beyond the comfort zone is new opportunity and growth. What you are feeling is not fear; it is excited anticipation for something new and unknown. What a gift to yourself to bring in new energy and new vitality to your life!

There is nothing unsafe, only unknown.

Baby Steps

The hardest part of taking action is not knowing what step to take. However, once you identify the first step towards your goal, the second step will appear, and the third and so on. If you want to empower yourself to get out of your comfort zone, come up with one small step you can take that is doable and not overwhelming. Can you make one phone call or send one email? Can you sign up for a class or recruit a friend? Maybe you need support in making a change; can you ask someone for help?

I know there is something you've been wanting to do, but every time you think about doing it, you stop yourself and convince yourself that the timing isn't right, or you need something more to be able to do it.

Stop holding yourself back and just take one baby step in the direction of what you want. It's the hardest step to take, but once you do, watch how your own excitement will propel you toward the next step. Pretty soon you will feel unstoppable.

Cultivating Resilience

Resilience is your ability to bounce back in the face of setbacks. (In many ways, we've been talking about it already.) Resilience is positive self-talk and encouragement when things don't work out as planned. It's the growth mindset that says everything is a learning opportunity and nothing is a waste. You tell yourself you may not know or be able to do something *yet*, but you will. Your ability to reframe a situation to see the benefits and opportunity for growth will help you build resilience and navigate the unpredictable twists and turns on the way to achieving your goals.

Summary

The goal of this chapter is to help you understand the importance of believing in yourself and developing your self-confidence. Confidence is the starting point for fully stepping into yourself and living the most authentic life possible. Hopefully now you understand this, and you realize that no matter where you are starting from, you have the power to increase your confidence and become unstoppable. Nothing happens and nothing changes unless you act. You have everything you need to escape the comfort zone. You can overcome your fear if you are willing to take small steps and support yourself with resilient self-talk and a growth mindset. Don't let yourself settle or stay stuck. You deserve to fulfill your potential and have, be, and do everything you want. I believe you can do it. Do you?

Step Three
Build Your Self-Confidence, Recruit Resources to Help you Escape Your Comfort Zone and Take Action

Action Plan and Exercises

Let's put these ideas down on paper. Go get your journal or Guide and take a couple minutes to yourself so you can reflect on these ideas.

EXERCISE ONE: I LIKE MYSELF

Here you can boost your self-esteem by making a list of at least ten things you like about yourself. They can be physical characteristics, personality traits, certain abilities, or achievements you are proud of. You can also make a list of what your partner or best friend would say if they were asked what they like about you. You are a valuable person, with unique gifts to offer this world, and only you can offer those gifts in your way. What are they?

EXERCISE TWO: CREATE A CONFIDENCE INVENTORY

This exercise will help you determine your strengths and see where you can improve. First, write down three to five areas where you feel confident and three five areas where you don't.

For each area of low confidence, come up with at least one action you can take to improve. For example, you could take a class, find a mentor, or practice a skill.

EXERCISE THREE: ESCAPE THE COMFORT ZONE

One problem with the comfort zone is that we don't realize we are there until we try to leave.

Take a piece of paper and draw a big circle to represent your comfort zone.

On the inside of the circle, write down all the activities you do that feel comfortable and safe, which might include your current job, relationships, and daily tasks. On the outside of the circle, write down three things you've been dreaming about but avoiding.

For each goal you are dreaming about, list a baby step you could take toward achieving it. The baby step has to be something so easy that you can easily imagine yourself doing it. It doesn't matter if it seems too small: any action is better than none.

EXERCISE FOUR: RECRUIT YOUR INNER CHEERLEADER

Recruit your inner cheerleader to combat any negative self-talk. Start by identifying any self-critical thoughts you've had recently about yourself ("I'm not good enough," "I can't," "I'm going to fail"). For each of these, come up with a positive affirmation and evidence that proves this idea wrong. For example, if your critical thought is "I can't," write: "I can, because I've overcome similar challenges in the past, and I know I can do it again."

Chapter 4

Have the Courage to Express Yourself: Communicate Clearly and Connect Authentically with Others

It is not about finding your voice; it's about using your voice.

I have learned that communication is all about translation. In order to have your needs met and get what you want, you have to learn how to translate your thoughts and feelings in a way that others will understand.

Growing up, I was a very sensitive child and had a lot of feelings. I was always trying to tell my parents how I was feeling and get them to understand what I was going through. Unfortunately, both of them were much more analytical in the way they understand the world, so all my talk about feeling sad or worried was like speaking a foreign language to them.

Don't get me wrong: they tried. My mother would try to associate each feeling with a bodily need. If I was sad, she'd suggest I was tired; if I was angry, she'd suggest a snack. Sometimes she was right, but most of the time I was just overwhelmed with feelings.

My father, on the other hand, would try to help me resolve my feelings by taking action. What did sad look like, and what would I need to do to feel happy? What would happy look like? When I felt anxious or worried, he would ask me what I needed to do to feel more in control. He did not believe it was helpful to spend a lot of time feeling the feelings. He believed that staying stuck in the feeling prevented you from moving forward: your goal was to determine the course of action that would get you through the feeling and back on track. He came at feelings from a logical perspective and saw them as obstacles to overcome.

One time when I was in high school, I had gotten into a fight with Nicole, my best friend at the time. I was upset and frustrated that she did not understand my side of the story, and I did not want to talk to her. I shared this with my dad, and he asked me what had happened. I explained that she and I had planned to go to a party but just before we were supposed to get picked up, our ride had changed their plans and was no longer going to the party. I decided to stay with the group and go along with the changed plans, but Nicole didn't want to, so she decided to stay home. She was angry at me for "abandoning" her and felt I should have stayed home as well.

I was simmering in anger and frustration. My dad suggested that rather than submitting to frustration, I take action and call her and apologize. He explained that if I took responsibility for my part of the circumstances—the choice to go out with the group rather than stay home—and acknowledge how that choice affected Nicole, I would be taking control of my feelings and I would feel less anxious. It would also make Nicole feel better, because I would be taking ownership of my actions and validating her experience. I took his advice and apologized. I did feel less anxious, and she did let go of the fight. We moved on as friends.

My parents had different ideas of what to do with feelings. My mother, one of ten children, had learned to turn feelings into physical symptoms with solutions. My father's way of dealing with feelings was to do something, solve the problem, and get away from it. They both grew up in a generation that did not appreciate the emotional experience the way we do now. As a result, I got really good at doing something with my feelings and really bad at embracing them and showing vulnerability.

Not expressing my feelings led to chronic stomachaches throughout my childhood and in college resulted in full-blown panic attacks. My boyfriend at the time (now my husband) suggested I explore what was going on with a therapist. In my family, you didn't see a therapist unless you were crazy or something was really wrong, so I had never even considered the idea. However, I was so overwhelmed I decided to give it a try, and I ended up with my first therapist.

Therapy transformed the path of my life. I learned how to name my feelings and gain the confidence to tell the people in my life what I was feeling and why. I got better at communicating my thoughts and feelings because I finally had a language that made sense to others. I could finally translate what was going on for myself in a way that people understood. I felt seen, validated, and empowered. I also gained a deep appreciation for the mind-body connection, since all those years of stomachaches had been messages from my body, and I would never ignore it again.

Up to that point, I had always thought I would follow my father's path, but this experience helped me to realize the value of being authentic. I realized that in order to achieve meaningful connection, you had to be able to communicate, and you can't do that if you don't understand yourself. I dedicated myself to helping people understand themselves and learn how to clearly communicate their thoughts and feelings to others. Clear, honest communication is a gift that builds meaningful relationships and a tool that leads to great professional success.

The Power of Your Voice

Your voice connects your inner world of thoughts and feelings with your outer world of relationships and interactions. The way you use your voice can either bring people closer to you or push them away. It has the ability to inspire change and encourage people to make a difference with their actions. It can make you feel loved, validated, understood, and appreciated. Your voice has the ability to teach and lead others to experience meaningful lives. It can enable you to protect those who can't protect themselves. Knowing how to use your voice and having the courage to do so is the foundation of communication and self-expression.

Your voice connects your inner world with your outer world.

Communication skills play a big role in personal fulfillment: your ability to clearly communicate what you need and want will determine whether those needs are met or whether you will feel unseen and unheard. The more you advocate for yourself, take responsibility for getting what you want, and recruit resources to help you along the way, the more of your goals you will achieve. Speaking up and making yourself heard is also a key to professional success.

In my therapy practice, it is just as important for me to listen as it is to guide. Through this exchange, I am able to understand and interpret what my clients are saying so that I can meet their needs and establish trust and connection. The same is true in any professional setting. Communication skills allow you to connect more meaningfully, feel more secure, and influence those around you.

Mastering self-expression through communication skills helps you meet your needs, because when you can clearly express your thoughts and feelings, others will know what you want. In exchange, when you can understand and interpret what others are saying, you have the ability to meet their needs, establishing trust and connection. Developing your communication skills helps you cultivate stronger relationships, because when you are vulnerable and share your feelings, it often allows others to connect with you more deeply. Relationships then tend to feel more fulfilling, secure, and trustworthy.

In fact, your ability to effectively communicate with others will determine the quality of your connections with the people in your life. Connecting with people is the only way you can influence them to take the actions you need or want them to take. Whether it's showing you more affection or buying your product, people are more likely to do what you ask them to do if they feel connected to you, because then they trust you. Good communication skills lead to greater connection, which leads to more trust, which leads to the ability to influence.

Your ability to communicate with others will determine the quality of your connections.

Whether you have chosen a path of corporate ambition, sole entrepreneurship, the role of traditional wife and mother, or countless others, your ability to influence is essential. You will need to influence and lead with confidence to be able to sell your ideas, whether it is a matter of motivating your team, promoting your products, or convincing your kids to get ready for bed. Your ability to influence and persuade gets things done. Communication skills empower you, deepen your connections, and inspire others to act.

The Art of Communicating and Connecting

Each person is unique, with their own set of experiences, perspectives, and ways of expressing themselves. You are unique: no one else is like you; there is only one you. You are the only person who fully understands things from your own perspective. The images you have in your mind are uniquely yours, and no one can see exactly what you can see.

This is important to understand, because in my decades as a therapist, I have worked with countless people who experience distress and frustration because they don't understand how the people close to them don't know what they are thinking. They find it disappointing that they have to express what they need, because their partners don't just read their minds. They feel the other person doesn't care, because if they cared, they would just know.

I want to save you this frustration and tell you that if someone close to you needs you to clarify what is going on in your head, it doesn't mean they don't care about you. Think about how often you change your mind or your understanding of something. Only you can keep up with what you are thinking all the time.

Imagine that your job in every conversation is, first, to assume the best intentions in the other person (people are generally good and helpful and want a collaborative conversation) and second, to set up each conversation for success. Each conversation is an opportunity to bring someone closer to you, collaborate on a common goal, or inspire someone to act.

My goal is to teach you communication skills that enable you to effectively share your thoughts and emotions and understand others. I want you to be able to express yourself clearly and understand what others say. I'm going to teach you my five C's of communication, which will empower you to have clear, effective, meaningful, and productive conversations with anyone in your life.

The Five C's of Communication
ONE: COMPONENTS

The first C is for the *components* of communication: the parts that you use to express your thoughts and feelings. There are three parts: the words you use, the tone you use to speak to them, and your body language.

Words represent ideas, concepts, and feelings. They carry vibrations that affect you. Positive, encouraging words help you feel strong, healthy, and safe. They are essential for you to feel confident in working towards your goals. At the same time, negative words can tear you down, causing you to doubt yourself and feel insecure about taking action.

The words we use are so powerful they can affect us on a cellular level. In 2018, Ikea, the Swedish furniture company, did an experiment in which they set up two plants in different areas. Both plants had identically controlled environments and received the same amount of water, light, and nutrition. For thirty days, they asked elementary school students to participate in the study by bullying one plant with insults while giving words of praise to the other. At the end of the experiment, the plant that had been bullied was noticeably smaller and more shriveled in comparison to the lush green leaves and vitality that beamed from plant that had received praise. The negative words said to the one plant caused it to shrink and lose vitality, whereas the plant that received praise was given support and encouragement to grow and flourish.

If words could have that kind of impact on those plants, can you imagine the impact they have on you and the people around you? You can build someone up or tear someone down with what you choose to say.

You can build someone up or tear someone down with what you choose to say.

Each word we use carries its own meaning—not a general meaning, but the meaning we assign it. You can never assume that your meaning or associations with a word is the same as someone else's. This is especially true for abstract ideas like *love*, *health*, *success*, or terms like *challenging*, *painful*, or *scary*. You can also change the meaning of a word or phrase with comparatively subtle alterations. I can't tell you how many couples I've worked with where the conflict arises because one partner answers with a "yeah" versus a "yes." Another example is how you experience the words when someone says to you, "Love ya" versus "I love you."

It is a good habit to seek to understand what something means to someone else, so it is easier to stay connected to them in conversation. When you are curious about another person's perspective, it shows respect and appreciation for differences.

Nevertheless, certain words do hold the same meaning across cultures, languages, and generations. These words carry such power that they can change the course of a conversation or alter the dynamic of a relationship. They are words that are easily used but often forgotten or avoided. Some of the most powerful of these are *please*, *thank you*, and *sorry*.

Please indicates a request, not a demand. It lets the other person know that they have a choice. When you add *please* before a request, you are showing the other person that you respect them and don't see yourself as above or better than them. You are asking them for help in some way, and using *please* activates the other's person desire to help. Every day, you find yourself in situations where you need help or collaboration from others—including your partner, your kids, your boss, your employees, even the barista at the coffee shop. Using *please* makes the other person feel important and valued, and when you make people feel good, they want to reciprocate and make you happy in return. You create a connection, if only for a moment.

Thank you offers gratitude and appreciation. It tells the other person that what they do matters and makes a difference for you. If using the word *please* begins the request, saying *thank you* acknowledges the time and effort it took the other person to meet the request. Demonstrating respect for the other person, saying *thank you* dissolves any sense of hierarchy between the two of you.

Sorry acknowledges distress and takes responsibility for the action that caused the distress. It tells the other person that their feelings matter and that you see them and have empathy for their experience. Just to clarify: no matter what the circumstances, you can always acknowledge that something caused another person distress. You may have done something unintentionally or even unrelated to the person, but your actions did cause distress. You are not admitting to hurting someone's feelings on purpose or that you are at fault, but by acknowledging that your behavior had a negative impact on another, you help the other person feel validated. When you tell someone you are sorry that something happened to them, you show empathy for their experience, and it makes them feel valued.

As you can tell, using the words *please*, *thank you*, and *sorry* can transform how a person feels emotionally. You have the ability to make the people around you feel good about themselves just by always using these words.

TONE OF VOICE

The second component of communication is your tone, or how you say the words you use. In fact, the tone of voice has more impact than the words themselves. Your tone has a vibration which will affect the other person before they even process the words. If you speak with a loud, fast tone, you will automatically command the other person's attention, but you will potentially put them on the defensive, because loud and fast sounds aggressive to many people. But if you speak slowly and softly, the other person is more likely to be relaxed and receptive to what you are saying.

Sometimes when I'm working with a couple that can't stop arguing, I tell them to whisper when they have sensitive conversations that typically turn into arguments. They often come back to me surprised at how well the whispering works.

Lowering your voice is also a great technique to diffuse an intense conversation, because people get louder when they become upset and reactive, so if you get louder, you will escalate the intensity. But if you speak more softly, the other person will start to match you and soften as well (obviously this doesn't work every time, but it does most of the time).

Your voice is like an instrument, and the way you play the tone affects how others respond to you and feel about what you say. Think about how you respond to different types of music. Some music makes you happy and gets you moving, and other music makes you sad, sleepy, or relaxed. Your tone of voice has the same impact as the tune or beat of a song.

BODY LANGUAGE

In the 1970s, psychologist Albert Mehrabian created the 7-38-55 rule. His research indicated that 7 percent of meaning is communicated through the words you use, 38 percent of the meaning is through your tone of voice, and 55 percent of what you convey is through your body language.

Thus your eye contact, whether you are smiling or not, and how you hold your arms tells someone how you feel before you even open your mouth. You know this: think about when you are sitting with a friend who, during a conversation, looks to the side or checks their phone. You feel frustrated and ignored, because their body language makes you feel unimportant. However, when they look you in the eyes and smile at you, it makes you feel valued and cared for.

In a conversation, crossing your arms gives the impression that you are defended and not open to new information. If you appear defended, the other person will automatically feel they need to defend in turn. However, arms that are open and relaxed give the impression that you are receptive, open to ideas, and not defended. As a result, you will make the other person feel more relaxed.

Your body language conveys a message to others, but it also has an influence on how you feel. In her book *Presence*, Amy Cuddy talks about the impact of the "power position" and how standing in this position—with your hands on your hips and a wide stance—boosts your confidence and makes you feel more powerful. Try this: shrink your body by crossing your arms and shrugging your shoulders and look at the floor. How do you feel? Now stand tall, look straight ahead, place your hands on your hips (like Superman), and push your feet firmly into the ground. How do you feel?

You can change your emotional state by changing the way your hold your body, and you can make another person more comfortable by demonstrating receptive body language.

Two: Consciousness

Becoming *conscious* is the second C in becoming a great communicator. Self-expression is all about communicating our ideas, needs, and wants to others. But before we can express our thoughts and communicate with others, we first need to communicate with ourselves. Hence consciousness.

To clearly and effectively communicate your thoughts and feelings, you need to know what you are thinking and how you are feeling. It starts by getting to know yourself better and increasing your self-awareness. It's like turning on a light in your mind to discover the way you think. Your attitudes and expectations of the world, your beliefs about yourself, others, and your values—what is important to you? When you listen to the voices in your head, what stories do they tell? How do you talk to yourself about other people? How do you talk to yourself about *you*? Remember the power of the words we hear, whether from others or from ourselves.

To communicate your thoughts and feelings, you need to know what you are thinking and how you are feeling.

The more we speak to ourselves with kindness and respect, the better we feel about ourselves and the more self-esteem and confidence we experience. The way you talk to yourself is often how you talk to others, so being kind to yourself will benefit the people around you as well. When you encourage yourself with positive self-talk, you build up your self-esteem and confidence, which helps you speak clearly, kindly, and with good boundaries. This sets you up for connected, collaborative conversations.

Part of communicating with yourself is being able to identify how you feel emotionally. You need to be able to identify if you are happy, angry, frustrated, scared, excited, confused, content, or anxious. Are you comfortable or uncomfortable? For most people, unclear emotions can be distracting and uncomfortable. In addition, emotions have a vibration: even if you can't identify them, you still feel them, and often the people around you can feel them too.

In my experience as a therapist, when you can name the feeling you're having, it dramatically reduces your feelings of anxiety or confusion. I call this "name it to tame it." By naming the emotion, you gain a sense of control over it and can then do something about it. Furthermore, after you name the feeling to yourself, you can name it to others. That will enable them to understand what is going on for you, so they don't take responsibility for your feelings. This is especially important in your close relationships with partners and kids, who are very aware of your feelings and can't help but be affected if you are distracted or overwhelmed because they dont know if they are responsible or have done something to upset you. Often the people close to you will feel anxious or upset if you are unable to name your feelings, and this can lead to confusion or misunderstandings. It can be helpful for you to identify the feeling you are having and tell the people close to you. For example, you can say I'm feeling anxious because I'm behind schedule on something. Clarifying this brings peoples closer to you as allies vs pushing them away.

By becoming more conscious of your thoughts and feelings, you can also determine what your limits are and set better boundaries. First, you identify how you feel, then determine what you need as a result of that feeling. At that point, you can ask for what you want or tell someone what you *don't* want. If you don't listen to yourself and take care of meeting your own needs, you can become frustrated and resentful and even become angry or passive-aggressive.

Sometimes my husband comes up with a plan in his head and decides he wants something, but he fails to tell us (we have three kids) or get our buy-in. Somehow he thinks that because he has made this plan, we automatically know his thoughts, and then all of a sudden he becomes frustrated because things are not happening. I have to remind him to think out loud and tell us his plan or what he needs so we can participate. When you have an idea in your head, it's up to you to effectively clarify it, first to yourself and then to others.

A big part of being conscious of yourself is the ability to listen to others. Just as you express yourself and want others to understand you, you need to accurately interpret what they mean with what they say. There are three aspects to this point:

1. **Always assume the best intentions.** If someone says something that hurts your feelings or causes a big emotional reaction, pause, check in with yourself, and wait to react. Notice what feelings come up for you.
2. **Ask for clarity.** Make sure you are interpreting what someone is saying accurately and based on their intentions. You can say something like, "Can you say that another way so I fully understand?" or "Can you clarify what you mean?"
3. Listen and **focus on what the other person is saying**, and then repeat it back to make sure you got it right.

Three Tips for Effective Listening

1. Always assume the best intentions.
2. Ask for clarity.
3. Listen and focus on what the other person is saying.

It's important to understand that you have total control of how you think and how you choose to interpret things. When you have positive thoughts and positive expectations of people and experiences, you will have positive feelings and enthusiasm about your interactions. The same is true for negative thoughts. Your job is to adopt the habit of positive thinking so you can communicate in a way that is collaborative, effective, and feels good to you and others.

Three: Constructing the Conversation

The third C is about *constructing* the conversation and how we create a framework for our conversations with others to set ourselves up for success. It's about being intentional and proactive by reflecting on what you want or need in advance and being mindful about what the other person may want or need from you. Constructing is about putting structure in place to support clear expression and accurate understanding. There are three techniques to help you build structure.

PREFACE THE CONVERSATION

A helpful technique for having an effective conversation is to introduce the idea of talking. For example, rather than just jumping right in with your question, start with "Can I ask you a question?" or you could say something like "I'm curious about . . ." This gives the other person warning and a sense of your intention. Saying something like, "I need to talk to you" often triggers people, who may well think they've done something wrong. Because they see you as coming from an offensive position, they automatically go into defense. You could even say something like, "I'm not mad, but I would like clarification about something." Your goal is to help the other person stay in a receptive state so you can ask your questions or share your ideas and the conversation is smooth.

In personal relationships, it's also helpful to be physically near someone if you want to discuss a sensitive topic. Taking the other person's hand or sitting next to them on the couch is a nonverbal way of showing that you come in peace and are a friend. Using the words *us, our, we* as a way to recruit your partner into the conversation is also much better than starting with *you need to* or *you should*.

In personal relationships, it's helpful to be physically near someone if you want to discuss a sensitive topic.

For distractable people, it's helpful to ask for a period of focused attention. You can say something like, "I need to speak to you for about ten minutes. You are not in trouble. When is a good time for you?" This allows the other person to eliminate other distractions in order to focus on you. I highly recommend leaving phones and similar devices in another room when you want to speak with a distractable person.

You can give a person an opportunity to be receptive to a conversation, but you can also ask for an opportunity to be present and able to talk. For example, you get home from work and as you're walking through the door you spouse or child comes running up to tell you all about something important that happened that day. You can tell them you are excited to hear all about it, but you need a couple of minutes in order to transition to being at home so you can give them your undivided attention. Prefacing the conversation is about setting the stage before you begin.

MANAGE EXPECTATIONS

We need clear expectations so we can feel confident in our actions. When we are confused by a request or a conversation, it causes anxiety and makes it harder to act. One of the best things you can do is to seek clarity from others and do your best to explain clearly what you want and need.

In general (there are exceptions), women and men approach conversations differently. Men are typically problem-solvers. When you go to talk to them about something, they immediately try to identify the problem and come up with a solution. Women typically want and need to verbally digest thoughts and feelings out loud and multiple times before they find resolution. If you want to share with your male partner, please tell him what you want from him. Tell him you just want to vent and need him to listen to you, or ask him to help you solve a problem. You will find that your communication will greatly improve, and you will both feel much more satisfied with your interactions.

Another thing about managing expectations and seeking clarity is relevant when experiencing "big" feelings: If you are having a conversation with someone and they say something that makes you feel bad or have a big emotional reaction, please ask them to clarify what they are saying or intended to say. I can't tell you how many times I've worked with a couple where one person has been misinterpreted, and as a result the other person has gone off feeling hurt and upset for days. Once we discuss the interaction and identify the misunderstanding, the feelings are resolved and the connection is restored.

There is no need to feel hurt if you can ask for clarity in the moment and feel resolved. This is relevant to any relationship. If you think there has been a breakdown in communication that you don't fully understand, or it appears that other person may not have fully understood, seek clarity. You can say, "Does what I just said make sense?" or "Could you clarify what you mean by that?" To prevent disconnection, take responsibility for not making something clear and state your intentions if you think you've been misinterpreted.

SET BOUNDARIES

Whenever you have a conversation, there is the chance that someone will ask you for something. In that case, you will have to answer with a yes, no, or maybe. This dynamic is very hard for some people, because if you want to say no, you may also feel that you don't want to disappoint the person asking you, or you may fear other consequences.

There are a couple of factors that make it easier to set boundaries. First, you need conviction. Say you have been asked to stay late or volunteer to take on some task. If you are planning to say no, you need to know why you are saying no and what you are saying yes to (such as family time or a friend's birthday dinner). By knowing what you are saying yes to, it's easier to say no to something else. In fact, whenever you say yes, you are also saying no. You are always making choices, it's just a matter of which one reflects your value system more.

Another response that you can give when someone makes a request is to tell them you will think about it and then determine whether you would be willing to offer something in response, and if so, what. For example, if someone wants you to take over a project, you could say, "No, I can't be solely responsible for the project, but I would be happy to be a part of team responsible for it." It isn't all or nothing: you can always offer something in between as long as it feels OK to you.

I once asked my dad about setting boundaries as a woman entering a professional setting, and he told me a story. It was relevant both to my situation at the time and to setting boundaries in any scenario. He explained to me that in farming, when they bring a herd of cows into a corral, the cows will walk the perimeter of the fence and every couple of feet, they will shove their bodies against the fence to see if it will budge. They continue doing this until they have made it all the way around and back to the gate. Once they confirmed that the fence was solid, they give up and move to the center, where they pasture.

Unfortunately, people are a lot like cows, especially kids and extra persistent people: they will bash into your fence, hoping to push your boundaries. However, if you stay strong and hold your boundary, they will eventually give up and stop pushing.

Four: Collaboration

The fourth C is *collaboration*. Ideally, you want to go into a dialogue seeking a win-win outcome between you and the other person. To do this, you have to figure out what they want so that when you try to get what you want, you can also make them feel happy with the outcome, since their needs are met as well.

Collaboration is all about understanding and appreciating differences. If you start with the attitude that there is no "right" or "wrong" way to do something, only "different" ways, it is much easier to negotiate, navigate differences, and achieve win-win communication.

People process thoughts and express themselves differently. Let's explore some of the common differences among people so you can learn how to be more collaborative.

People process thoughts and express themselves differently.

EMOTIONAL VERSUS ANALYTICAL

Some people are led by their heart and come from an emotional place when processing information and expressing thoughts and feelings. For these people to hear and understand you, you first have to connect with them emotionally. If you are resolving a conflict or trying to agree on a decision, you start by addressing how they are feeling (whether positively or negatively) before proposing any logical ideas. You might ask, "How does that make you feel?" You would not justify your actions or explain yourself before you address the other person's emotional experience. In other words, their feelings need to be validated (meaning that you understand and appreciate them) before they can open their mind to practical thoughts and action.

Analytical people like to understand a situation or idea from a logical perspective. They tend not to get excited or too emotional about something until they can fully understand it in a linear, rational way. This is why often one person gets very emotional or excited about something, while the other stays neutral or even-keeled. It's not because the latter don't care; it's because each has a different emotional expression, pace, and range. It can be hard trying to collaborate given this difference. I've worked with many couples where an emotional person is married to a logical person. Sometimes even though the logical partner wants and tries to understand, they can seem disconnected, as if they just don't get it. Not to mention how frustrating it is when the emotional partner is very excited about something and the logical partner doesn't match their level of excitement. For the logical partner, it feels like a daily roller coaster with emotional ups and downs, while the emotional partner feels they are dealing with a round of predictability.

INDIRECT VERSUS DIRECT

Indirect communicators tend to express themselves more passively. They often suggest or share an idea that has multiple interpretations, whereas direct communicators are clear in their communication but can come off as demanding. Indirect communicators tend to process internally and think about an idea quietly in their minds, whereas direct communicators are external and quick to express their thoughts or feelings. The indirect communicator wants to share their answer once they have concluded about it, while the direct communicator comes to a decision after sharing their entire thought process out loud.

Here is an example of being indirect versus direct. A husband says to his wife, "Honey, we are out of milk." The wife hears him stating a fact, while the husband thinks he has just clearly asked his wife to go get more milk. I have a joke in my house, because my husband will often say, "We need to . . ." I will turn to him and ask, "Is this a 'we/me' or a 'we/you?'" If it's a "we/me," I know he will take on the task; if it's a "we/you," I know he expects (or hopes) that I will take action. It also saves us a lot of frustration.

Sometimes indirect communicators take longer to make choices, which can be frustrating to direct communicators. If you are a direct communicator, you can offer a couple of choices to the other person, so they don't have to come up with the answer; they just choose the one they like best. This way, they still have an option and are participating, but a decision is made at a faster pace.

I'm sure you've had the experience of going out to dinner with a friend or partner, and one person will ask, "Where should we go for dinner?" The other will say, "I don't know. Where do you feel like going?" This back-and-forth can continue for several rounds.

One way to approach this problem is for one person to suggest two or three options and then let the other person decide which one they prefer. The person offering the choices is suggesting options they like, and the other person gets to choose which one they like best. It ends up as a win-win for both.

PRESENT VERSUS FUTURE

You may also come across the difference between present-oriented people—people who operate in the moment—and future-oriented people, who commonly have a range of times for taking action. Let's say a present-oriented person asks a future-oriented person to perform a task, like making a phone call or taking out the trash. The future-oriented person might agree to the task but thinks it can be performed within a reasonable amount of time: they will say yes and plan to complete the task sometime that day, whereas the present-oriented person is expecting the task to be completed immediately. I'm sure you can imagine the frustration when these two people are in a relationship.

Another variant has to do with time: one person sees time as precise, while the other person sees time as a range. You make plans to meet someone for dinner and tell them you will meet them at 7:00 p.m. One of you believes the time to meet is 7:00 p.m. sharp, and it would be rude and disrespectful to be late. The other sees 7:00 p.m. as a target to aim for, and it's perfectly fine to show up between 6:50 and 7:10.

If you are the kind of person who sees time as a suggested range, I highly recommend that you tell others that you will meet them within a certain range and never commit to a precise moment. You will save yourself a lot of disappointment and prevent a great deal of frustration for others.

This idea ties into what I said earlier about managing expectations: if you tell the other person what to expect, they will feel respected and will be more collaborative. If you don't manage expectations, the other person feels disregarded, which affects connection and communication.

RECIPROCITY AND EQUITABLE EXCHANGE

Relationships are based on constant negotiation. You are offering something to the other person, and they are offering something to you. You want to offer something that they want and need, and you are hoping to get something you want and need. Earlier I said you are selling your ideas, and in truth we are always selling something; it just depends on what you sell and to whom. You may need to convince your colleague to take on a job or complete a project. You may need your partner to give you more affection or help out more at home. You may need to convince your kids to cooperate with a plan they don't like. In every case, your goal is to express yourself—your thoughts and feelings—in a way that creates connection and buy-in from the other person. They need to know they will get something out of the deal.

In the best relationships, you feel that you get out what you put in. When you feel you are putting in more time, effort, or energy than you are getting back, you will inevitably start to feel resentment and disconnection. The same is true if you are taking more than you are giving, except that in this case you are the one causing resentment.

In the best relationships, you feel that you get out what you put in.

An equitable exchange occurs when the value offered is the same as the value received. Yet very rarely in relationships do we offer the same item of value that we take in return. For example, in a marriage, one person may be responsible for earning money while the other may be responsible for managing children and supporting the home. Both people offer essential value, but not in the same way. As long as the arrangement feels fair, there is an equitable exchange. *Fair* does not mean *same*: it's apples and oranges versus apples and apples.

ASK YOUR WAY TO SUCCESS

One thing my dad has said to me for my whole life is, "The answer is always no unless you ask." You want to develop the confidence to ask your way to success. Ask people for their advice. Ask people what they think of your ideas. Ask them to help you. Ask them what you can do to move ahead. But be prepared to ask. And don't forget to ask others what you can do for them.

Most people are reluctant to ask for fear that they will be turned down. But you will find that all truly successful people are unafraid to ask for the help, support, or the advice they need. You will be surprised at how willing people are to be of service.

Five: Consideration

The fifth C is *consideration*. Making the effort to consider another person is one of the most powerful things you can do. You may consider someone after they've done something for you or in advance of something you will do that affects them. In either case, your consideration will tell that person that they matter.

OFFER APPRECIATION AND SHOW GRATITUDE

We all work hard to make the people in our lives happy. You want to do a good job at work, so your colleagues, employees, or boss are happy with your contribution. You want to do a good job at home with your partner, your kids, and even your pets, so they feel cared for and thrive. You want to be a good friend and provide support and companionship. No matter where you invest your time and energy, you want to know that it matters. Nothing tells you that more than when someone tells you they appreciate you and your effort, and they say thank you. Offering gratitude is a gift. It often transforms the idea that the other person "has to" do something to the idea that they "get to" do something.

THE FIVE LANGUAGES OF APPRECIATION

Offering appreciation can go beyond just saying thank you. You can offer meaningful appreciation by giving someone something that matters to them. In his book *The Five Love Languages: The Secret to Love That Lasts*, Gary Chapman talks about the five different ways people give and receive love.

> **Five Ways of Showing Love**
> 1. Words of Affirmation
> 2. Gifts
> 3. Acts of Service
> 4. Physical affection
> 5. Quality Time

I tend to see love as appreciation, and there are different types of appreciation. You can usually identify your primary love languages by how you tend to show appreciation, but it's important to learn how others want to be appreciated. You can appreciate someone with words of praise. Tell them what you like about them and their efforts and how they have affected you.

You can also appreciate someone with a gift. Depending on the context, give them flowers, a bonus, or something they can unwrap to tell them you've thought about them. The gift represents your appreciation physically.

Another way of showing appreciation is some act of service. You can bring someone lunch, take care of a task at work, or do some extra housework to show you appreciate the other's effort.

You can also offer physical affection with a hug or cuddle on the couch or some other act that connects you physically (although I don't suggest doing this at work).

The fifth way to show appreciation is to give the other person your undivided attention and spend quality time with them. Focusing your attention on another person shows you are willing to give them your most valuable asset: time.

Never miss an opportunity to make another person feel important. My favorite quote is from author Maya Angelou: "People forget what you said, people forget what you did, but people will never forget how you made them feel." You can have a great impact on the people in your life by making them feel good about themselves and the value they offer. Many people measure their worth by how much others need them or how much they can do for others. Take the time to tell the people in your life that they matter and their efforts mean something to you. The more we build up the people around us, the better we become as a whole.

Summary

Here are the five C's of communication, which will help you have connected, collaborative conversations with the people in your life:

1. **Components.** Be aware of the words you use, the tone you use to speak them, and your body language.
2. **Consciousness.** Self-awareness, knowing your thoughts and feelings, will set you up to clearly express yourself so that you can get your needs met and understand others.
3. **Construction.** Setting up the conversation for success and using a framework to establish boundaries ensures that you will have more productive, satisfying interactions with others.
4. **Collaboration.** By learning how to navigate differences, manage expectations, and striving for reciprocity, you will stay connected in relationships and achieve more.
5. **Consideration.** Say thank you and make sure the people in your life know that they matter to you.

The Five C's of Communication

1. Components
2. Consciousness
3. Construction
4. Collaboration
5. Consideration

Step Four
Apply the Five C's in order to Communicate Clearly, Express Yourself and Connect Authentically

Action Plan and Exercises

Now let's apply these ideas to your life and see how you can improve your communication and connection with others.

Here are some reflective questions to help you:

1. What kind of tone do you typically use when speaking? Loud and fast, or slow and quiet?
2. Is your self-talk kind and positive or are you hard on yourself? What can you eliminate from your inner dialogue to make room for more positive encouragement?
3. Which of these styles do you identify with: emotional or analytical, direct or indirect, present or future?
4. How do you feel about your ability to set boundaries with others? What boundary would you like to set? Plan to do so by incorporating the techniques from this chapter.
5. What is your love language? When others want to show appreciation, which form means the most to you? Commit to telling this to three people you are close to. Ask them which love language they relate most to.

Chapter 5
Harness Your Unique Value and Find Purpose in Everything You Do

IN THIS CHAPTER, WE will talk about how everyone comes into this world with some kind of natural talent. Imagine unlocking a superpower you've carried since birth and could use to change the course of your life. I'm going to help you figure out what your natural talent is and how you can make the most of it.

When I was first reflecting on this idea, I went back to my childhood and traced what I believe to be my natural talent. People have always come to me to help them understand something that feels complicated. As a child, I was fascinated with where babies came from, and once I learned all about the miracle of life, I felt compelled to teach anyone and everyone who would listen—to the point that I was nicknamed "Dr. Ruth" in first grade.

At first, I thought I had a natural talent around understanding sex and intimacy, but I continued to trace the evolution of my work and remembered how in college, I became passionate about psychology and communication. I made every effort to help my friends and family better express themselves and live more authentically in their relationships. I taught them all about feelings and interpersonal dynamics. That path continued, and I earned a PhD in human sexuality, elevating my knowledge in both intimacy and relationships and allowing me to continue to teach people how to have more meaningful connections and experience greater pleasure in their relationships. The theme of me as a teacher continued.

Simultaneously, I have been working with my father in the field of personal and professional development. We have written three books together, and I cofacilitate his public speaking academy, where I have the opportunity teach people how to organize their thoughts and express themselves in an authentic, effective, and engaging way. Much of what I do with the speaking academy participants is to hear what they want to say and help them reorganize their ideas so that what other people hear is what they want to convey. I help them synthesize and simplify their ideas so that they can teach others. I also do this as a coach and have helped many clients develop their own coaching programs or workshops designed to teach skills and ideas. If I had to define my natural talent, it is that I have the ability to understand complex ideas and translate them into simplified terms so that others can understand.

Today I employ this talent as a speaker teaching personal and professional development; as a couples therapist, translating thoughts and feelings from one partner to another; and as a coach helping others develop the curriculum for their own programs. I'm good at synthesizing information, and I combine that talent with my passion for teaching and empowering others with knowledge and skill.

I think I inherited this skill from my father, because I've explored his work. What makes him successful is that he is really good at taking a lot of information, simplifying it, and reordering it in a way that makes it easily understood. He does this with business concepts, and he is passionate about helping people make more money. The more he uses his talent to help others become more successful professionally, the more fulfilled and purpose-driven he feels.

For me, I can see how I use my talent both personally, with my family and friends, and professionally, as a therapist, speaker, and coach. Across every area of my life, I teach people by simplifying complicated ideas. The more I empower people with knowledge, the more fulfilled I feel. Using my skill makes my efforts and contributions feel more purposeful and satisfying every day.

The Power of Passion

Defining your natural talent, unique gift, or innate strength is the first step to unlocking your potential and feeling true fulfillment. You can use your strength to create positive change, whether by excelling in your job, contributing to your community, or developing a product or service and starting your own business. When you discover and develop your unique value and combine your skills, passions, and ability to help others, you connect to your purpose in a whole new way. By harnessing your unique value, you open up unlimited opportunity for success in life and work and feel truly fulfilled with all that you do.

Unfortunately, many people go through life never fully realizing their unique talents. Those that do often fail to embrace their potential and end up living lives that could have been so much more. Some people follow paths dictated by the desires of others (such as joining the family business) or are influenced by societal expectations rather than their own personal passion. As a result, they never fully embrace their potential or offer their real gifts to others.

True success comes from knowing and using your natural abilities to create a meaningful impact in an area you are passionate about. This could be as simple as being passionate about your children's health and cooking healthy organic meals for them, or as grand as being passionate about world hunger and starting a nonprofit organization to bring food to people in poverty. This kind of passion gives you a sense of purpose and drives your actions. Whether it's cooking a meal or putting together a presentation to investors, knowing the purpose behind your actions gives you a unique feeling of satisfaction when you complete them. Everything you achieve that is fueled by your passion and aligned with your natural abilities sets you up to live a fulfilling life.

True success comes from knowing and using your natural abilities to create a meaningful impact in an area you are passionate about.

In this chapter, I'm going to help you identify your unique value and recognize the natural talent or gift that is already present in you. I will help you understand your strengths and passions, so you can be clear about the purpose behind what you do. You will learn to appreciate your own effort in a new way. You will see how aligning your skills with your passion will bring more meaning to everything you do. We will also explore how you can develop your unique value and apply it in different areas. Whether your goal is to use your gift at home with your family, to contribute to your community, or to create a tangible offer from which others can benefit, you will learn the steps to harnessing your gift and finding greater purpose in all that you do.

What Is Your Natural Talent?

You have a natural talent. There is something you can confidently say that you are good at. It doesn't matter what it is, but it does matter that you can clearly define the unique value you have to offer. You need to know your strength and be able to tell others what it is before you can do anything actionable with it.

What do I mean by *actionable*? I want you to decide where and how you want to use your gift. You can only do that if you know what that gift is to begin with.

Define the unique value you have to offer.

Think about where your gift shows up right now in your life and how it impacts the lives of people around you. If you are a woman who considers yourself as a giver and invests a lot of time and energy doing things for others, it can be hard to see the deeper value in what you do.

In earlier chapters, we have talked about the importance of setting specific goals, so you know *what* specific achievements you are working towards. We've also talked about being proactive with your time and choosing your actions in advance, so you can determine *how* you spend your valuable time. Identifying and seeing how you use your gift will endow your actions with a greater sense of purpose. You will also develop a new appreciation for your efforts because you are tapping into the *why* behind what you offer. Once you identify what you are meant to offer and start to use it with purpose, you will transform your life in many wonderful ways.

Throughout this chapter, I'm going to go back and forth between the terms *natural talent*, *gift*, *strength*, and *unique value*, but they all refer to the same thing. You may connect more with one term more than another; besides, I want you to hear the idea presented in different ways.

Now let's figure out your gift. Start by thinking about your life story. What did you love to do as child? Did you play with dolls, build towers with Legos, hunt for bugs in the yard? My dad says that you can tell what a person is going to be when they grow up by the type of play they engage in as a child. He believes that you can see a person's gift from a young age and that our natural talents emerge in our hobbies and play as children.

Our natural talents emerge in our hobbies and play as children.

When I was little, I would spend hours playing with dolls. I would arrange my dolls in a row on my bedroom floor and pick each one up, one at time. I would hold the doll in my arms, lovingly feed it a bottle, and gently pat its back for an imaginary burp. I would change its diaper and wrap it up in a blanket and rock it to sleep. I would then lay the doll back on the floor and pick up the next one. It was pretty clear that I was naturally a nurturer and was preparing for motherhood from the time I was four years old.

I was also known as a chatterbox and spent hours talking to people wherever I went. I wanted to know everything about everyone, and I always felt compelled to share the stories I had learned. I walked around with a little blue Casio radio that hung from my shoulder with a thick canvas strap attached to a microphone. I would hold it up so I could announce the important information to whichever audience was present. I loved teaching people information, and whenever I learned something new, I would have to teach it to someone else. I was also a natural synthesizer of information.

If you can't remember that far back to childhood, take yourself back to high school. I have a dear friend who loved giving advice in high school. She was always talking to people about their romances, friendships, and how to deal with their teachers or parents. Friends would even consult with her about decisions regarding school and what classes they should take so they could get into college. She loved helping people find solutions to their problems. People were drawn to her because she made them feel comfortable. She ended up studying psychology in college and becoming a therapist. She found a way to dedicate her life and career to helping people solve their problems.

You can also look back on the things you've accomplished in your life thus far and reflect on those successes. What about your personality or abilities helped you achieve those wins? One of my clients, Mary, ran a marathon. When she reflected on that accomplishment, she remembers that in order to train for it, she had to be really good at time management. She had to juggle her work with school pickups and doing her training runs. She stayed focused on completing tasks one at a time so that she could be efficient and get more done in less time. Her strength is her ability to focus and organize her time in a way that maximizes her day.

Sometimes it's easier to ask other people how they perceive us. Ask your friends, family, or colleagues what they see as your strengths. People looking in from the outside see things differently than when you are on inside looking out. When I want people to identify a gift that seems hard to pinpoint, I will ask them how their best friend or partner would answer if they were there and asked about a strength. Most of the time, they are able to answer without having to ask the other person. So I ask you: what would you best friend say is your greatest strength or unique talent?

I was once in a workshop where the speaker asked the group what we believed we were good at; he called this special talent or skill our "superpower." I like the idea of having a superpower, because it bring your awareness to the one thing that you yourself feel the proudest of. The woman next to me said her superpower was that she was a "connector." She believed her gift was her ability to bring people together who could mutually benefit from each other's skills, resources, or insights. Another woman said she was really good at organizing: her gift was that she had great spatial awareness. She had the ability to rearrange the physical objects in a space, whether it was a closet, kitchen, or office and make it look and feel more functional. Her friends were always coming to her for help with organizing. In fact, thinking about what people come to you for is a great way to identify your natural talent.

Another way to recognize your strength is to think about what comes naturally to you. What activities are you drawn to because they bring you joy and fulfillment? These tasks excite you and make you feel energized; you may even lose track of time because you get so engaged in them. I like to think of these activities as things that charge my battery and give me energy.

Harness Your Unique Value and Find Purpose in Everything You Do

What do people compliment you on or rely on you for? Maybe you have a brain with a knack for numbers and a love for Excel spreadsheets. People come to you to help them organize information or calculate a budget. Are you a good communicator? Maybe you love to volunteer to make announcements or lead meetings. You might even love to give speeches or talks in front of people. (Yes, since public speaking is a major fear, that is a gift.) Maybe you are a good writer and have mastered the social media platforms with your engaging posts and compelling stories.

There are many kinds of gifts. You are born with some of them, and you develop and cultivate others through education and experience. Whether your special talent is an actionable skill, like writing, cooking, or organizing, or you've identified something more abstract, like communication, leadership, or persuasiveness, you most definitely have a unique value.

You are born with some gifts, and you develop and cultivate others through education and experience.

Fuel It with Passion

Once you get clarity on your natural talent, the next thing to explore is your passion. Passion is the fuel that drives and directs our actions. You can be passionate about many things, but combining passion with your natural talent gives you a sense of purpose. For example, Emily is an excellent writer, and she is passionate about education, so she helps high-school seniors write college essays so they can get into universities. Nicole has great leadership skills and is passionate about being an involved mother, so she runs the parent organization at her children's school. Paula is a great cook, and she is passionate about the benefits of a plant-based diet, so she opened a food truck and travels around the city bringing delicious vegan food to the community.

Exploring what you are passionate about will help you determine how to use your gift, because once you figure out what you can do, you will need to decide where and how you want to do it. I also think it's important to know what you care about and where you want to make a meaningful impact. Sometimes we get caught up doing all kinds of mundane daily things and forget why we are doing them.

I was recently talking with a woman named Beth, who shared with me how frustrated she felt because after work, she would come home to her husband and kids, and immediately following dinner, she would find herself cleaning and organizing the house. We talked about why she felt compelled to clean and organize the house. She explained that she had done research on how the environment affects your stress levels, and she was passionate about having a home that made her family feel relaxed. After we talked through this, she realized that there was purpose in her actions: she wasn't just compulsively cleaning every night. When she realized the impact it had on both her and her family, it completely changed how she felt about the act of cleaning and organizing her house. When you change the way you think about something, it changes the way you feel about it.

Where Do Your Passion and Skill Intersect?

Many people focus on what they can do and find opportunities and jobs where their skill is needed and valued, but often they focus too much on using the skill and not enough about where they are using it. That's why it is so important to find where your skills and passion intersect. You want to be using your skill in an area that matters to you.

This book is all about getting you to define success for yourself. Part of that is determining your skill, what you are passionate about, and where those two intersect. Where do you want to direct your abilities? This is a deeply personal choice, and determining it will make a great deal of difference to your sense of fulfillment.

It's important to note that at different times in your life, you will find yourself passionate about different things. As a young woman, you may be focused on your desire to advocate for the environment or become a career woman. When you become a mother, you might change and instead care more about parenting and attachment. And when your children are older and independent of you, you may find your passion in yet another direction, such as mentorship or health. Women are constantly reinventing themselves at each stage of life. Your talent and natural abilities will come with you on the journey. You can use them in each phase based on what you feel passionate about at that time.

Start with where you are right now. Decide what you feel passionate about. What would be a good use of your talent? Where do your passion and skill intersect? Where can you make a meaningful difference? You can apply your skills to excel in your job and cultivate your professional development. You can focus on your homelife, offering your talents to your family and children. You can contribute to your community and apply your skills to local initiatives. You can also take your gift and start your own business.

Turning Your Gift into a Tangible Offer

We've been talking a lot about how you can find more fulfillment in your life by applying your natural talents to what you are passionate about. You can also take those natural talents and develop them into a high-value skill that allows you to offer something tangible to others. Imagine if you could take what you love doing and transform it into a business that makes money.

This is why I have emphasized clearly identifying your gift in order to make it actionable. Once you make your gift actionable, you can develop it and choose how you use it or sell it.

First, explore your special skills, which are often abstract like communication, problem-solving, creativity, or leadership. Then you make them actionable by making them into something marketable. For example, you can take a skill like writing and turn it into something tangible, like a blog or a newsletter. You could create a writing class or coaching program for aspiring writers. You could even write your own book.

Next, you want to refine your gift into a high-value skill. You want to improve your craft, so you will need to practice using the skill. You will want to get feedback from your peers, family, and potential clients as you begin to think of how you can develop and improve your offer. Take classes or attend workshops so you gain more information and learn from other people who have taken a similar skill and turned it into a business.

Refine your gift into a high-value skill.

Harness Your Unique Value and Find Purpose in Everything You Do

In fact, looking at people who have succeeded in the area you are interested in is the best way to develop your own business. If someone has discovered what steps to take to achieve the results you want to achieve, ask them how they did it, and do the same. That is why so many people are out there promoting proven "systems" and "formulas": it isn't necessary to reinvent the wheel. Just find out how other people have done it, and then add your personal approach to make it yours.

Here is an example: you know a lot about fitness and health. If you want to organize that knowledge into a tangible product or service, you would first develop the skill by getting certified as a personal trainer or nutrition coach so you have some credibility in the field. You could then build up a network or establish yourself by sharing workout tips or health hacks on social media. You could also start a YouTube channel and create a series of videos. Once you've gotten yourself known, you could create a coaching program and sell it to people who like your approach to fitness and health and want the results you can get them. You define your offer through the results you can help others achieve.

Here is another example: Nancy is really good at organizing. At first, she was asked by her friends and family to come and organize their kitchens and closets. She loved to do this, so she decided to start a business where she would sell her organizing services to people. In order to turn her talent into a tangible offer, she first had to identify her system. What steps did she take when she helped people organize? In order to do this, she needed to continue recruiting people she could help so she could record her process. Gaining clarity into her process would provide her with a formula to follow with each client, and she could improve this formula by getting feedback at each step. She could also use positive comments as testimonials to the value she provides. This helped her build a foundation and portfolio for her business. Again, the goal is to transform your unique value into something tangible that achieves results from which others can benefit.

Packaging Your Gift into a Marketable Offer

Hopefully now you have an idea of what value or result you have to offer. The next step is figuring how to deliver those results. You could sell a service or a product or contribute to your community or nonprofit organization.

Is your offer service-based? When you offer a service, you are selling your ability to achieve or help someone achieve a specific result. Maybe you have special knowledge in business, personal development, or parenting, and you want to offer a coaching or consulting service to help people improve in these areas. You could also offer your services as a freelance contractor and provide writing, graphic design, or social media management. Another type of service is teaching or training, whereby you create online courses, workshops, or offer tutoring. If you wanted to sell coaching, you would offer individual sessions or create a package that includes a series of sessions aimed at achieving a specific result.

I work with a couple of different freelance graphic design artists who run their own businesses. I hire them to create digital products like logos, book covers, and other digital elements or to design and manage my website. All of these are examples of providing a service.

Is your offer a product? Maybe you can make things like jewelry, clothing, or artwork. If so, you can build a business around these. If you are good at photography, you could sell a photo shoot and offer a series of photo packages or products. You can also sell digital products like e-books, templates, and other printables. One woman created a series of printable activity sheets to help children enjoy learning certain concepts in elementary school. She started an online business and sold her sheets through Etsy, a small-business platform. Another woman created "self-care" boxes for busy women and established a business based on selling subscriptions for her curated boxes. There are many subscription-based businesses selling products, ranging from exclusive content to deliverable items like foods, holiday boxes, and even relationship enhancement kits.

Community-based or nonprofit contributions are opportunities to donate your time and abilities. Here you can showcase your ability to organize, establish collaborations, or start specific groups or initiatives. You might organize a workshop, a mentorship program, or an event targeted to community needs. There are always opportunities to help create partnerships that support local businesses and neighborhood schools. Taking the initiative to bring about awareness, change, or new structure to the community is a great way to bring value.

There are many examples of how women have used their skills and passions to create incredible businesses. Joy Cho was a stay-at-home mom who started a blog as her creative outlet, and it became the lifestyle brand and business Oh Joy! Or Sara Blakely, who started her shapewear business from home and built it into Spanx, a brand that has transformed women's fashion. How about Reshma Saujani, a female entrepreneur who took her love of science and founded Girls Who Code to empower young women in science? Starting and running your own business gives you a lot of flexibility.

Many women have used their skills and passions to create incredible businesses.

If you are looking to use your talents in meaningful ways, feel valued, and still keep life balanced at home, consider starting small. Choose to offer your services to a select few, or create a small batch of products to sell to the community or at the local farmers market. Taking the first step is the hardest, but if you can push yourself to take the leap and you want your own business, take action. There are so many opportunities out there for you to monetize your expertise.

Summary

In this chapter, we explored your unique value and how to recognize the natural talent or gift that is already present in you. We talked about how passion fuels your actions. When you find where your talents and skills intersect with your passion, you release your potential for greater fulfillment and purpose.

Identifying how you are using your skills to contribute to your family or share with your community can transform the way you view your efforts. Remember, when you change how you think about something, it changes how you feel about it. Hopefully now you can identify where you are already using your gift.

We explored how to take your gift and transform it into a tangible offer that you can market and sell. First, you learned to identify the talent and clearly define it. Then you discovered how to make it actionable by describing the results you can achieve with it. Next, we saw how your clarity about delivering those results sets you up to build a business, big or small. Now it's up to you to decide if that's you want and go for it.

Step Five
Identify Your Unique Value and Decide How to Use it

Action Plan and Exercises

Now, go get your journal or guide and get ready to explore these ideas.

EXERCISE ONE: DEFINE YOUR NATURAL TALENT

What do you excel at naturally? (For example, creativity, leadership, spatial awareness, communication.)

What do you people frequently ask you for help with? (For example, organizing, design, advice, technical skills.)

How does your talent help others? (You help them solve a problem, save time, improve their lives.)

EXERCISE TWO: USING YOUR TALENT

Where are you using your natural talent? Can you use it more intentionally?

EXERCISE THREE: WHAT ARE YOU PASSIONATE ABOUT?

Determine what you are passionate about and focus on your purpose.

Whom do you care about helping or serving in some way?

What causes or missions do you feel strongly about?

What brings you joy and engages your passion?

EXERCISE FOUR: WHERE TALENT AND PASSION INTERSECT

Where do your talent and passion intersect? How can you use what you are good at in a context you feel passionate about?

EXERCISE FIVE: CREATE YOUR TANGIBLE OFFER

1. Define the results you can achieve with your natural talent.
2. How do you achieve those results? Is it through a product or a service?
3. Identify who benefits the most from those results.
4. Where do you find those people?
5. Write out a description of what results you get and who benefits from those results. Start telling people what you have to offer.

Chapter 6
Redefine Success in Motherhood

THERE IS NO ONE way of feeling accomplished. That means there is no one way of defining success in motherhood. Motherhood plays a significant role in the lives of many women and can have a profound impact on how we determine our success. Women experience motherhood in many ways and with varying degrees of involvement, from staying at home to working full-time to everything in between.

For my whole life, I knew I wanted to be a mom. At a certain point, I also knew that I wanted to have career and pursue my ambition. For as long as I can remember, I've been in constant negotiation between the two. Sometimes when I find myself celebrating the wins in one area, I feel guilty that I've slacked in the other.

There is no one way of feeling accomplished.

In college, I made the choice to pursue a career in psychology so that I could slowly build my business while having kids and being an available mother. I've worked hard earning several degrees, establishing a private practice, writing books, speaking internationally while volunteering as a room parent, making dinner, and staying involved in my children's school. To this day I have special dates, or "hangouts" as my son prefers to call them, with each of my three children every week, and I make them a priority above all else. As a mom, I've discovered that if your kids are OK and happy, you are free to be happy too. When your kids are struggling, it makes it nearly impossible to focus on your own ambitions.

Overall, I think I've done a good job of cultivating both tracks. However, whenever I spend time with my father, he tells me how proud of me he is for marrying such a good guy and raising happy kids. I think, "What? Yes, I've been really invested as a mother and I have a great husband, but what about all the other things I've achieved with my profession?"

I know that he knows all that I've done with my career, and I know that he is proud of those achievements, but he never highlights them; he always focuses on my domestic achievements. I've reflected on this, and I know that in his generation, success was measured by a man's ability to provide for his family. If his wife had to work, it sent the message that he wasn't making enough money for her to enjoy the luxury of not having to work.

Of course, we women know that staying home to take care of the house and raise the children is in fact a lot of work, but many men who are primary breadwinners have no idea how much goes into keeping a home. Even my super supportive husband, Damon, did not appreciate the task until he took some time off and stepped into that role so I could focus on my work. Finally, the jokes he made about me having free time during the day while the kids were at school came to a screeching halt.

My father's focus on my role as wife and mother somehow made me feel that he didn't value my professional accomplishments. Even though I know how hard I've worked, he sees success for me in my role as a mother and wife. I say this because I believe this is a common attitude. It may be a generational narrative that continues to influence perceptions today and suggests why it might be difficult for women to give themselves credit for everything they do and appreciate what they are capable of. We've come a long way, but it still feels as if the value you offer is easier to measure in dollars than in happiness and well-being.

Accomplishment, for me, is inseparable from my experience as a mother. Your definition of success might also be profoundly influenced by how you value motherhood and measure your achievements with your children. When most women become mothers, there is a major shift in what they want from their lives. Often, you enter this world of motherhood and lose yourself there, gradually starting to add back pieces of yourself until you feel whole again. At that point you may look around and have a completely different attitude regarding what you want and what you care about. You have to define success in motherhood to have a compass and give yourself credit for that part of your life.

Motherhood Is a Vital Part of Success

Traditionally when we talk about women's success, we tend to focus on what they have accomplished professionally, not how they've navigated motherhood. Can you imagine if parenting was recognized as an achievement? That would be incredibly empowering to many women who dedicate a period of time, or most of their lives, making that their primary responsibility. How can we recognize motherhood in its many shapes and forms as a barometer of success? What if mothers could be acknowledged for taking on the responsibility in the first place and valued for the time and care dedicated to parenting their children into adulthood?

Most societal definitions of success overlook motherhood and undervalue what it takes to dedicate yourself to the role. Even if society isn't there yet, we can define success for ourselves. Each one of us needs to validate the importance of that role, which is a key measure of accomplishment for many women. Since motherhood is a major part of most women's identities, it needs to be incorporated into a modern, holistic vision of success.

Define Success in Motherhood for You

To have a fulfilling experience as a mother, it will help you to define what success looks like in that role. It doesn't matter if you are not yet a mother or if you've been on the motherhood journey for a while: it is always valuable to pause and think about what kind of mother you are or want to be. Then reflect on whether you are living (or believe you can live) those ideals. For me, it was always important to have a deep relationship with my children so that they felt comfortable enough to trust me and share things with me. I've worked to achieve that mothering value by making sure to spend quality one-on-one time with each of my kids, so we have had the opportunity to cultivate relationships. I've also felt strongly about my children's relationship with one another and have seen myself as the facilitator of their connection as siblings. I've worked hard to teach them how to communicate (using their words, not their bodies) and navigate issues. I've also prioritized opportunities for them to spend time together and learn how to rely on one another in different circumstances. Obviously, it's not always perfect harmony, but when I look at how they get along, I feel happy and satisfied.

Part of defining success for you is aligning your parenting goals with your personal values. One of my primary values is building self-esteem. As a result, my husband and I have made it a goal to help our children develop high self-esteem. We believe that a big contributor to self-esteem is feeling connected to the people in your life and having a good social network. As a result, we always make big decisions through the lens of what will most support their self-esteem. It is how we choose schools and camps, where we set boundaries, and how we navigate social dynamics.

Align your parenting goals with your personal values.

A good friend of mine has a different primary value in parenting. She holds academics as the most important value. All of her major parenting choices have been made through the lens of what is the best academic path for each child. How will each decision affect their academics? She has made choices that I would never have made, and I have made choices she never would have made.

It's important to evaluate what is important for yourself as a mother and let others choose their own path. There is no right path, only what is right for you and your family.

In determining what success looks like for you, it could be helpful to think of other mothers whom you admire and what they do that you appreciate. What about them as mothers would you like to emulate? You can also think about what you've experienced or observed from other mothers (including your own). Think about what they did that you want to do with your children and what they did that you don't connect with. Remember, not good or bad, just different.

Having a guide for your parenting journey based on the goals you value will support you so that you can check in and see all that you've achieved. Did you do what you wanted to do? Are you the kind of mother you strive to be? Have you facilitated the kind of experiences you want your children to have?

Motherhood can be all-consuming. It's easy to get lost in the process and feel that you haven't achieved great things. But when you identify the targets of your motherhood journey, every time you achieve one, you will feel a sense of satisfaction and can keep track of your wins.

Being Present for Your Children

The distractions of modern life have made it incredibly challenging for mothers to stay fully present with their children. Presence is about giving your children your full attention in both big and small moments. It means putting away distractions and being emotionally available. It's about creating opportunities for connection so you are there for those important windows of time. Believe me, I know, in this fast-paced world, it can be tricky to seize those opportunities and fully show up.

There are two kinds of presence: physical presence and emotional presence. Physical presence is showing up. I remember how important it was for my kids to see me at school events and how aware they were of the parents who never came. I also remember the struggle of not being able to show up for everything and the guilt that comes with feeling I was letting them down. I know I'm not alone in this, because all the time, I hear from women who are trying their best to be present with their kids while fulfilling all other responsibilities.

When it comes to showing up, all you can do is your best. Decide what moments you need to be there for, and ask your kids what is important to them. Don't be afraid to tell them you can't be there, and manage expectations. It's better for them to know you won't be coming than to hope you'll show up and be sad when you don't.

> *When it comes to showing up, all you can do is your best.*

Now you may be the kind of parent who shows up for everything and is always available for your kids, but the one time you didn't show up is the one they talk about. You have to cut yourself some slack and do the best you can to show up when you can.

I've decided for myself what would feel good to me, and as a result, I plan my schedule in such a way that I can drive my kids to school and pick them up a certain number of times per week. When I'm able to achieve that goal, I feel good about being physically present in that way. It's helpful to have measurable goals so you can validate your efforts.

The second kind of presence is emotional. You can show up everywhere all the time, but if you're distracted and unable to emotionally connect with your children, they feel it. It's not just quantity: it's the quality of the time you spend together. You have opportunities to be present with your kids, like breakfast in the morning, bedtime at night, and whenever you are in the car together, but if you are multitasking with work or stressed out and distracted, you miss those moments for connection. Kids spell *love* T-I-M-E, so look for everyday opportunities for connection and ways to be present. You never know which small actions will have the most impact.

It's important to set boundaries with work or other commitments, not just for your children, but for you. People often ask me how I get so much done and still manage to spend quality time with my kids. The secret for me is to have self-discipline and be fully present when I'm working and then shift gears and be fully present when I'm with my kids.

Another thing you can do is set boundaries for yourself and stop working at certain times. Stop checking email or returning calls and be present at home with your family. I also plug my phone into the charger in the kitchen at a certain time and leave it there for the rest of the evening. Setting a physical boundary with your phone helps you disconnect and shows your kids that you are available.

When I was a young child, my father would start his day sitting in his big brown chair, drinking coffee and reading the newspaper. I would quietly walk up and stand in front of him on the other side of the big, open sheet of paper. He would peek around the side and see me standing there, and he would immediately fold up the paper and put it to the side so he could give me his full attention. Sometimes I would talk to him, and sometimes I would smile and just run away, but without fail he made himself available to me. To this day, I still remember how special it made me feel that he would stop what he was doing to prioritize me.

I keep this in mind now as a mother of three and try very hard to do things that show my kids, they are important. In his book *Twenty-Five Ways to Win with People*, John C. Maxwell talks about how you can't always choose the moments that will be the most important, so you have to make the most of the time you have and be present. This will increase your chances of catching that important moment. Take advantage of the opportunities you have. You never know what will make your kids feel important.

Cultivating Healthy Family Relationships

Strong relationships are built on trust, consistency, and emotional safety. This foundation helps your children feel secure and valued. Your job as a mother is to contribute to creating a secure base for your children so they have the confidence to go out and explore and grow as individuals while knowing that you love them unconditionally and will always be there when they get back.

Your job as a mother is to help create a secure base for your children.

We know from attachment theory (first defined by John Bowlby and Mary Ainsworth) that your relationship with your child will shape their emotional and social development. This in turn will impact both their self-esteem and their ability to form and maintain relationships. When you are a responsive parent and do your best to be available and meet your child's needs (most of the time), you cultivate a secure base for your child. Your child learns to trust that they can explore and be curious. They understand that sometimes things work out and sometimes they don't, but when they don't, you are there to help soothe the distress. They learn to tolerate distress and become more resilient. They also learn to trust you and feel secure in their connection with you.

Building Trust

You can build trust with your children by being consistent, reliable, honest, and vulnerable. Children (and many adults for that matter) are very intuitive. They can pick up on how you are feeling despite the words you use to describe your state of mind. It's important to be authentic with them and own your feelings. Tell your kids when you are worried, angry, or sad, and share a reason so they don't take reasonability for your feelings. For example, if you are worried about a friend's health, you can tell them you feel worried for your friend. Or if you are angry at your partner, you can say that you feel angry because your partner did something you did not like. You want them to learn that it's OK to be honest about having uncomfortable feelings. You want to teach them how to express their emotions. You also want to create a safe space for them to share both the good things and the bad things with you. You want your children to know they can always be honest with you and that you love them unconditionally.

Another one of my parenting values is honesty. We have a rule in our house that if you tell the truth, you won't get in trouble. I'd take credit for this rule, but it was a rule I grew up with, and it never made me feel afraid to tell the truth. I learned that mistakes happen, and you take responsibility for your mistakes, you don't hide from them. Being able to tell your parents when you've made a bad choice and have them not shame or reject you for failing at something gives you the opportunity to be authentic in your relationships. It also makes you less afraid of making mistakes. That has a powerful lifelong impact.

As a mother, I try to be honest with my kids and own my mistakes to help them know that it's OK. I once heard someone say, "If your kids feel the need to lie, who has made it feel unsafe to tell the truth?" I've thought of that on my parenting journey, because I don't want my kids to feel they need to lie. I want to be a safe space for them so they know they can always come to me for support and acceptance.

If your kids feel the need to lie, who has made it feel unsafe to tell the truth?

Discipline and Structure

As both a therapist and a mother, I have found that people thrive with boundaries, frameworks, and containment. Humans need to feel a sense of containment; they need to know that they can have emotional experiences that won't consume them. By this I mean that in life things happen that cause big feelings, and those big feelings can take over and feel overwhelming and out of control. We often need help containing those feelings, whether it's our own internal dialogue reminding us that we will be OK or a loving voice that helps us name the feeling and process it so it becomes more manageable.

As a mother, you have the opportunity to be that loving voice to help your children name their feelings and feel more in control.

Often, we as mothers also need to name our own feelings and tell ourselves it will be OK before we can help our children do the same.

My dad told me about a great metaphor for setting boundaries as a parent. He said our children are like plants, and the boundaries we set as parents are the pot. We create stability and parameters for growth by determining the size of pot, the amount of room our plant needs, and the depth required to create strong roots. Our parenting involves sunshine and water to nurture the plants, but we also reinforce the framework. Some children need us to guide and motivate them with consequences; some children thrive better with rewards and incentives. Each child is different, but in either case they need a solid framework so they can thrive and grow tall and strong.

The Five Love Languages

I've already mentioned the book *The Five Love Languages* by Gary Chapman, which goes into depth on the different ways people give and receive love. As I mentioned in the earlier chapter on communication, the five ways of showing love (or appreciation) are words of affirmation, quality time, acts of service, gifts, and physical touch.

I frequently ask my children what their love language is (sometimes it changes) and if they feel they are getting enough love from Damon and me. They will tell us; they enjoy being able to use this as way to express their need for more love. We also share our love language with them, so they know how to show appreciation for us. It's a great way to introduce the idea of appreciation to your children. It's also a helpful tool to guide you as a mother so you know that your efforts are having an impact.

Balancing Ambition and Family Life

I strongly believe that having your own ambition outside of motherhood is healthy and important. There are many ways you can continue to cultivate your ambition while navigating motherhood. Although it requires balance, intention, and flexibility, making a commitment to always having something that is for you—whether it's a profession, a hobby, or a place where you invest your time and energy—will help you feel independent and connected to your own identity beyond that of motherhood.

I've watched many women become mothers. They lose themselves in the role, and later on, when their kids are more independent of them, they struggle with not being "needed" as much. They find it challenging to reconnect with themselves and find a new purpose or to clarify what they want.(Often their focus shifts to the relationship, and this can be a challenging time for couples.)

It's also challenging for women who have had careers to suddenly shift their priorities and focus solely on their children. On the one hand, it feels great to be fully invested in your family, but on the other hand, it becomes harder to reenter the work force or even know what kind of work you want when you decide to go back. Even for a lot of women who had been focused solely on their careers, the idea of going back full-time doesn't feel ideal anymore; finding a new kind of work-life balance is more appealing. In any case, being able to balance your work and your family life is crucial for integrating your ambition with motherhood.

Women are historically incredible multitaskers and often fall into the trap of trying to get everything done all at once. However, if you are committed to pursuing your ambition while having a rewarding family life, you have to have a plan for balancing those roles. It will require focus. You have to set boundaries and create schedules so you have structure while remaining flexible when the inevitable unexpected need arises. Learning how to stay focused on the task at hand is the secret weapon to being more efficient in either role. First, you establish your intention and then focus on work, or you choose to be present and focus on mothering. Not only will you get more done, but you will also feel more satisfied with what you accomplish.

Several time-management strategies can help you balance your ambition with family responsibilities. A great way to start is creating a schedule that both considers the time you need for your ambition and protects the moments you need to feel good as a mother.

Once you have a schedule, cultivate your self-discipline and stick to it by getting really good at saying no to things that take you off course. Make sure also to ask for help from the people around you. Remember, no one does it alone; it takes a village. We all need support from others, especially from other moms. Find ways to take turns and reciprocate so you can support and help one another achieve your respective goals.

Now let's talk about challenging the "mom guilt" narrative in regard to ambition. You do not need to choose between success and being a good mother. One of my biggest motivators in writing this book is to tell you that there is no one way of feeling accomplished. As we've seen, there is no one way of defining success in motherhood. You choose for yourself, and as long as you are being proactive with your own choices, it is right for you.

You do not need to choose between success and being a good mother.

The guilt feeling is inevitable. I have not yet met a mother who did not relate to the idea that when she wasn't invested and focusing on her children, she felt guilty in how she spent her time. She felt guilty going out to dinner with friends and missing bedtime; she felt guilty going out to town and missing the soccer game. She felt guilty being at the office and not at home when the kids got home from school. For whatever reason, there is a part of being a mother that makes you feel compelled to be available for your children, often at your own expense.

Nonetheless, invest in yourself, and demonstrate to your children that you have value to offer beyond mothering. Remain passionate about making a difference or pursuing your own ambition. In this way, you teach your children that you are a person beyond being their mother. You give them something to respect, admire, and strive for.

Navigating Common Challenges

If you've ever been on an airplane, you know that when they give the safety talk, they always tell you to put your oxygen mask on first before putting one on anyone else. They tell you this because if you pass out from lack of oxygen, you will not be able to take care of anyone else.

This is as true for motherhood as it is for airplanes, yet one of the biggest challenges for mothers is finding time for themselves and giving themselves permission for self-care and mental well-being. In my practice, I've often suggested to a mother that she needs to schedule a "me" day and set aside several hours where she can do whatever she wants without feeling bad about it. If you schedule time for yourself and embrace the opportunity to decompress in whatever way works for you, you will be more present and will feel greater fulfillment when you are with your family. Investing in your mental well-being will also prevent motherhood burnout. You need time for yourself. The easiest way to have it is to proactively schedule time for yourself that doesn't sacrifice family moments. This is where asking for help from other people really comes in handy.

Mothers also struggle with the feeling that they are not doing enough. One reason for this is that it is impossible to ever finish the to-do list, because it is constantly growing. Mothers also struggle with this issue because they compare themselves to other mothers. We are constantly being inundated with idealized portrayals of motherhood on social media. How can anyone keep up with the perfect images you see on a daily basis?

Even if you are not comparing yourself to the online images and stories of motherhood triumph, you might feel the pressure to be the same as other mothers: the mothers in your social group, the wives of your partner's friends, the moms at your children's school, the stories you hear at the office, your mother-in-law, or your own mother. There are countless opportunities for you to compare yourself to someone else.

The truth is, no two people are the same: your experience and circumstances are unique to you, just as every other mother has her own story and her own circumstances. If you can accept that there is no "right" way to do it, you can give yourself permission to not be perfect.

I love the concept first identified decades ago by D.W. Winnicott, a British pediatrician and psychoanalyst who studied the mother-child relationship and came up with the "good enough mother" theory. He basically said that you cannot be a perfect mother, but your children do not need you to be perfect: they need you to be "good enough" so they can learn to be cared for while learning to tolerate disappointment and frustration in order to develop into happy healthy adults. Your goal is to strive for "good enough" and give yourself credit for all that you do.

You cannot be a perfect mother, but your children do not need you to be perfect: they need you to be "good enough."

Summary

Motherhood is a powerful, multifaceted journey that deserves to be recognized as a vital form of success. It demands presence, intention, emotional depth, and unwavering commitment. Whether you are a full-time mom, balancing a career, or somewhere in between, your efforts matter deeply. By defining success on your own terms, aligning your parenting with your own values, and creating strong, trusting relationships with your children, you are shaping the future. Balancing ambition with family life isn't just possible: it's necessary for your growth and fulfillment. Let go of perfection, embrace being "good enough," and remember to nurture yourself as you nurture your family. In doing so, you will not only raise resilient, connected children, you will also honor your own identity and purpose as a mother and a woman.

Step Six
Redefine what Success Means to you in Motherhood

Action Plan and Exercises

Now, let's take a moment to explore the following exercises. Go get your notebook or Accomplished Woman's Guide and do the following exercises.

EXERCISE ONE: CREATE A MOTHERHOOD SUCCESS STATEMENT

This exercise will help you reflect on what success in motherhood looks like for you. It will serve as a guide for setting goals and checking in with yourself when you need validation or guidance.

Get your journal or Accomplished Woman Guide. First, write down your top three values as a mother (such as connection, growth, kindness, structure, or independence). Then, using those values, write a personal Motherhood Success Statement, such as: "Success for me as a mother means raising emotionally resilient children who feel safe, loved, and free to be themselves." You would then describe what that would look like in action. For example, "My children are confident to walk into a new environment and curious to explore the room or talk with new people."

EXERCISE TWO: MOTHERHOOD ROLE MODELS REFLECTION

This exercise is meant to help you determine traits and actions you admire in other mothers that may inspire or guide you on your own motherhood journey.

Get your guide or journal. Think of two or three mothers you admire (these could be either people you know personally or public figures). Write their names down.

List what you admire about their parenting style or the impact they've had on their children.

Journal about the following prompt: *what aspects of their approach do I want to bring into my own motherhood experience?*

EXERCISE THREE: TRACKING YOUR PRESENCE JOURNAL

The purpose of this exercise is help you track and gain awareness of when you are physically and emotionally present with your child or children. You can keep track and make an effort to show up as much as you feel is important for you.

Get your notebook or journal.

For one week, take a moment every day to log one moment when you were fully present with your child, and one moment you were distracted but wish you had been more present.

At the end of the week, journal about the following: *What helped me stay present? What distracted me? What could I change or do differently next week?*

EXERCISE FOUR: CONNECTION INVENTORY

This exercise is to help you strengthen your connection with your children and teach them how to communicate their language of appreciation.

For each child, answer the following questions:

How do they best receive love? You can teach them about love languages (physical touch, words of affirmation, quality time, gifts, acts of service) and see which one they choose. Make sure to ask them for an example so you fully understand what they believe is their love language. You can also tell them what your love language is.

When do you feel most connected to your child? What are you doing? Where are you?

What one thing can you do this week to show love and appreciation and strengthen your connection?

EXERCISE FIVE: IDENTITY BEYOND MOTHERHOOD INVENTORY

This exercise will help you reconnect with your personal identity, creative passion and/or ambition. The idea is to make sure that you are investing in yourself while navigating motherhood.

Get your notebook or journal and answer the following journal prompts:

How would you describe yourself outside of being a mom?

What are three things that you are curious about or would love to spend more time doing?

If you had a one-week paid vacation for only you, and your children would be cared for by someone you trust and they like, where would you go, and what would you do with your time?

Chapter 7
Your Relationships Determine the Quality of Your Life

I'VE ALWAYS LOVED INTERACTING with other people and learning about them. I was that kid at the pool who would walk up to a child of a similar age and declare, "Hi, I'm Christina. Do you want to be my friend?" In fact, I made two friends on vacation when I was eleven, and both ladies ended up as bridesmaids in my wedding fifteen years later.

I have always enjoyed friendship and have learned how valuable it is to be in community with other people. Our connections are important. I believe that's why the art of relationships has always been a passion of mine and is one of my core drivers in all the work that I do. I'm passionate about helping people meaningfully connect with others, and I truly believe that the quality of our relationships determines the quality of our lives.

Growing up, I learned that my dad always approaches his relationships with the attitude of how he can help improve the other person's life in some way. Everyone tells me how kind and generous he is with his time and any resources that he can offer. I've watched how grateful people are when he shares time and wisdom with them. He is called to help others become more successful through personal and professional development. I feel driven to help people know themselves so they can authentically express themselves and experience meaningful relationships. We've had many conversations about the purpose of life and what brings people meaning. We both agree that, at least for us, being able to serve or help someone in some way is a great gift and makes life feel purposeful. I believe your relationships are constant opportunities to help or serve others and brings you joy.

My dad also taught me that you should take every opportunity to boost another person's self-esteem and make them feel important. He has emphasized that the most significant word to a person is their name. When you learn a person's name and call them by it, you make them feel important and respected. I've watched him do this with almost every person he meets. Whether we are at a speaking event or having dinner in restaurant, he always begins by asking a person's name and then he repeats their name to make sure he has it right. You watch as the person's face lights up and their posture shifts when they've been acknowledged with their name. It's a great way to start a relationship.

Take every opportunity to boost another person's self-esteem and make them feel important.

The Influence of Relationships

The people in your life have more influence on you than almost anything else, and your relationships with them will determine the quality of your life. Positive, healthy relationships can empower you, support you, and give meaning to your experiences.

Think about it: when something exciting happens or you achieve something important, you want to share it with someone you know will be proud and encouraging. When you feel sad or confused, you rely on the people who will support you and help you feel better. Your family, your friends, and your community give you a sense of belonging and a feeling of being a part of something beyond yourself.

Success is not achieved alone. Your relationships play a critical role in both personal and professional fulfillment. Strong, supportive relationships fuel your emotional well-being and give you more confidence to take on challenges and experience more joy in celebrating your wins. These are the relationships you want to cultivate and reinforce.

Relationships can also be tricky. There will always be people that will try to hold you back or make you question yourself. These people can ruin your day, hijack your focus, and distract you from what is important. However, becoming aware of these dynamics and resisting the negative influence of others is something you can learn. You can also learn how to navigate relationships with tricky people. Fortunately, some difficult relationships can be avoided, but some of these people might be in your family or in your workplace and are unavoidable. That is why it is so valuable to become confident at setting boundaries.

The goal of this chapter is to teach you how to cultivate deeper connections, manage difficult relationships, and set good boundaries. You will also learn how to build and strengthen your personal and professional networks.

Relationships That Matter

There are several kinds of relationships that matter. They are essential for you to feel successful and fulfilled. Your relationships with your partner, your family, and your close friends give you emotional and social support that helps you feel confident and grounded.

In an earlier chapter, we talked about having a secure base and that establishing it depends on having consistent, supportive, trusting, and reliable relationships. You need those kinds of relationships to give you a solid foundation from which you can explore and express yourself confidently. That solid, secure base also enhances your resilience and your ability to bounce back after failure. The best kinds of relationships are reciprocal, so you also want to be consistent, supportive, trusting, and reliable with the people that matter in your life so they too can experience that secure base.

Professional relationships help you develop in a different way. Whatever career path you choose, you will benefit from cultivating relationships with mentors, colleagues, clients, and collaborators. Although you have incredible potential and unique gifts, developing those gifts will require help. Your professional network can be a great source of support, information, and opportunity.

Cultivating Friendship

The basis of both personal and professional relationships is some degree of friendship. To help you cultivate better relationships with people that matter, we are going to use the acronym FRIENDS, which will remind you of what you can do to accomplish this goal.

The basis of both personal and professional relationships is friendship.

The FRIENDS Formula

F: Foster trust.

R: Respect.

I: Invest time and energy.

E: Express appreciation and gratitude.

N: Navigate conflict.

D: Develop mutual support.

S: Share experiences.

F: FOSTER TRUST

One of the easiest ways to build trust with other people is to be honest and vulnerable yourself. It takes a leap of faith to put yourself out there and reveal your imperfections. However, you will find that the fastest way to deepen a relationship is to demonstrate to the other person that you are not perfect. It gives them permission to accept their own imperfections. From there you can develop an authentic relationship based on full transparency and acceptance.

Although this is a simplification of what might take time to establish with someone, you can start small and share small vulnerabilities (like feeling worried or unsure of something) to see how they respond. Trust is not built overnight: it takes many small moments to create a deep friendship, but the more authentic you are, the easier it will be to trust you. When you create a safe space for sharing feelings and experiences, you easily foster trust.

R: RESPECT

In friendship, it is important to honor personal boundaries and accept differences in opinions, values, and lifestyles. Some people find it hard to trust their own choice when someone else makes a different choice, fearing that one is right and one is wrong. But if we can learn to embrace the truth that there are no right or wrong choices, only different ones, we can confidently make our own choice while respecting and appreciating those of another person. After all, when you go out to dinner with someone, you don't expect them to order the exact same thing as you. Life is like one big dinner: everyone gets to order what they want based on their own appetite, dietary restrictions, and preferences. When you allow others to express an honest opinion or need without judgment or criticism, you make it safe to be authentic, and your relationship deepens.

I: INVEST TIME AND ENERGY

One of my favorite sayings is, "You get out what you put in." That couldn't be truer for relationships. Spending quality time with people tells them that they matter to you and that you are invested in them. Consistent efforts to build and maintain a friendship will create a strong, meaningful relationship. The more you put into the relationship, the more you will get out of it.

Most relationships fall apart when one person begins to feel that they are putting in more time and effort than the other. This creates resentment. Make sure you are not always the one who initiates plans or extends yourself by accommodating the other's schedule or location. Ask for reciprocity and give them a chance to respond. If you happen to be the one putting in less effort, start taking the lead and showing the other person that they matter.

E: EXPRESS APPRECIATION AND GRATITUDE

People want to know that they matter and that what they do matters. Your friends, family, and partners play an important role in the fulfillment you feel. Make sure you acknowledge them on a regular basis. Tell them you appreciate them, the relationship, and the role they play in your life. Express gratitude, say thank you often, learn what their love language is (to remind you: words of affirmation, gifts, affection, acts of service, quality time), and use it.

N: NAVIGATE CONFLICT

Misunderstandings are inevitable in any relationship. The important thing is to consider the other person when you respond. There is a big difference between *reacting* and *responding*. Responding is a result of pausing and being intentional, whereas reacting is often impulsive and based in raw emotion.

Of course, if someone says or does something that hurts or angers you, you will most likely have an emotional reaction. However, if you can adopt a curious mindset and learn to assume the other person's best intentions, it makes it easier for you to be thoughtful and seek clarity before responding to any frustrations. Considering where the other person is coming from and being curious to understand the situation before jumping to conclusions helps you address disagreements with empathy and patience, so that you can understand and resolve any issues. Always seek a win-win situation with people, so everyone feels good.

D: DEVELOP MUTUAL SUPPORT

One gift of friendship is having a person who not just supports you but challenges you to be the best version of yourself, so you can continue to grow and embrace your potential. These relationships can be either personal or professional. When a relationship is based on trust and mutual respect, individuals are more inclined to receive guidance and take advice.

One of my closest friends is the person I go to when I want an honest answer about something I'm doing or want to do. She has always been brutally honest with me and challenged me to take more responsibility for my choices, good or bad. Sometimes it can feel harsh, but because we have such a solid foundation as friends, I know that she is coming from a place of love and acceptance. Her advice and friendship are invaluable. I'm grateful to have her support and the opportunity to grow with her.

When you are a dependable friend who provides support during times of need or encourages growth, it contributes to strengthening the connection. Throughout your life, you will either grow together in your relationships or grow apart. The only way to grow together is to push and support each other to have more, be more, and do more.

S: SHARE EXPERIENCES

The more you have in common with someone, the stronger your bond will be. The more memories and meaningful experiences you share together, the more you will have in common. I'm the oldest of four, and my parents take the whole extended family (all eighteen of us) on a vacation together every year. Travel has been one way my parents have facilitated shared family experiences. When we get together, even if we haven't seen one another for months, we can tell stories, reflect on past trips, and unite in those shared experiences. Our travel together has acted as a bond that keeps us connected, even though we have our own lives and families in different places.

For many women, motherhood is a shared experience and often creates an immediate bond, even in new relationships. In addition, having the same background, going to the same school, or overcoming a similar obstacle are other ways women bond and connect. It's amazing how powerful it is to share an understanding through common experiences or mutual triumph.

Let's summarize how to cultivate deeper, more meaningful relationships. At the heart of any meaningful relationship, whether it's romantic, personal, or professional, is a real friendship.

The FRIENDS acronym is a great way to think about how we can deepen those connections. It starts with *fostering trust*, which means being honest, open, and even a little vulnerable, so people feel safe being themselves around you.

It's also about *respecting* each other's needs, boundaries, and differences. Understand that not everyone will see or do things the same way, and that's OK. Relationships take effort, so consistently *investing* time and energy shows people they're important to you. Don't forget to *express appreciation*, because everyone wants to feel seen and valued. When conflict happens (and it will), try to *navigate* it with consideration: respond instead of reacting, and give the other person the benefit of the doubt. Real connection also comes from *developing mutual support*: helping each other grow and being there during the hard times. Finally, don't underestimate the power of *sharing experiences*: the more memories you build together, the stronger the bond becomes. These suggestions will hopefully help you invest in your friendships in a whole new way.

Setting Boundaries for Relationship Success

Boundaries are a part of any healthy relationship, because they foster respect and mutual understanding. You need to set boundaries in your relationships in order to protect your emotional and physical well-being and show up as the best version of yourself.

There are three kinds of boundaries: personal, professional, and emotional. You set *personal boundaries* to honor your emotional, mental, and physical capacities in your interpersonal dynamics. If you don't—if you are not honest with yourself about what feels OK—you will ultimately give too much and will burn out. To set your relationships up for success, you need to know what you are comfortable giving and receiving (in terms of time and energy) so that you can be authentic and feel good with others.

You set *professional boundaries* to help you manage your work-life balance. Professional boundaries can also be seen as how you divide your time and energy between your home life and your outside activities with work, community, and friends.

These days, it has become much more challenging to establish professional boundaries, because many people work from home. Moreover, with technology, we can be reached anytime anywhere, so it really does fall on you to set your boundaries in order to protect your personal time and relationships.

Finally, we have *emotional boundaries*, which tend to be the hardest type of boundaries to set. Emotional boundaries protect your feelings and mental health from negative influences and dynamics. These boundaries are harder to set and maintain because they come from an emotional place: it's not merely a matter of logistics, like determining an amount of time or saying yes or no to a task. Emotional boundaries involve choosing your well-being over the needs of others and coming face-to-face with someone else's disappointment. It's challenging for most of us.

> **Three Kinds of Boundaries**
> 1. Personal
> 2. Professional
> 3. Emotional

How to Set Boundaries

Now let's talk about how to set boundaries. The first thing to do is determine what you need, emotionally, mentally, or physically. You may need someone to respect your desire not to talk about an upsetting topic. You may need to protect your time alone after work before engaging in social activities. You may need to say no to any more commitments in order to have the mental space to achieve all your current tasks. You start by being clear about what you need before you can ask for it.

The second thing to do when setting boundaries is to openly and directly communicate with assertiveness. You don't need to be aggressive, but it is important to use clear, respectful, and direct language when expressing your boundaries. In most cases, you are not giving someone what they want, so there will usually be pushback. You can make it easier on yourself if you start by being clear and firm. You can use "I" statements to avoid blaming and reduce defensiveness. For example, you could say, "I can't take on any more commitments this week, but I can help next week," or "I feel overwhelmed when I'm asked to do things at the last minute. I'd appreciate more notice next time," or "I'm happy to spend time with your parents, but I'd rather have lunch with them, not dinner."

Next you listen for a response and anticipate pushback. Setting boundaries is hard for most people because others are usually disappointed when you say no or you don't agree to give them what they want. People feel guilty when they make someone sad or disappointed, and it's hard to stay strong when you feel bad for the other person.

Relationships are a constant negotiation made up of give-and-take and compromise. Compromise is established with boundaries. When you notice disappointment, it can be helpful to acknowledge the other person's feelings and say something like, "I understand that you don't like this change, but I need you to respect that it doesn't work for me the way it is." You can validate that the boundary feels frustrating, rejecting, or disappointing. That's OK. It can feel that way to the other person and still be a good boundary for the relationship.

Relationships are a constant negotiation made up of give-and-take and compromise.

Be prepared to defend your boundary. You will probably need to repeat and stand by the boundary when it's challenged. When you are consistent and restate it in a calm way, people will eventually accept that you are not willing to change your mind

Remember my example about the cows and the fence, keep a strong fence. Here is another example: think about when someone is trying to sell you something and is pushing for an answer.

Most of the time they are trying to sell you their idea or their plan. You might just say no, but you might have to add something like, "I've already told you no and that I need time before committing. I can't decide right now." You may need to repeat this multiple times.

One trick to feeling more confident in boundary setting is knowing why you are setting it in the first place. You can be clear about what you need, but you also need to be clear about *why* you need it. What happens if that need is not met either for you or for someone else who may be affected? Sometimes when we think about the impact on others, it is easier to stay strong. For example, if you are overwhelmed with commitments and you agree to take on an additional task, you will be taking time away from your partner or your kids, or you will be forced to sacrifice your own self-care. When you say no to something, you are saying yes to something else. Always know what you are saying yes to, so you fortify your ability to say no. Here is an easy way to remember how to set a boundary: think of being BOLD.

Be clear about what you need.

Openly and directly communicate with assertiveness.

Listen to how the other person responds, and be prepared to restate your boundary so you can

Defend your needs.

Dealing with Tricky People

You will inevitably have relationships with people who will challenge you, try to hold you back, and cause you stress. Confidence in setting boundaries is really helpful when you have to deal with tricky people.

We talked about cultivating meaningful relationships with friendship. Now we will talk about navigating the challenging relationships by controlling what we can control, setting boundaries, and learning to detach from the negative influences of tricky people. Who are the tricky people in your life? Those who are draining or unsupportive or diminish your emotional and mental well-being. You know what I'm talking about: that person who, when you see them or anticipate seeing them, gives you a sick feeling in the pit of your stomach. You can't wait for the interaction to be over. Or it's the person you spend time with, but afterwards you feel drained and full of self-doubt.

Tricky people are those who are draining or unsupportive or diminish your emotional and mental well-being.

First, make a list of all the people you regularly interact with that cause you frustration or distress. Then identify what they do that triggers emotional discomfort or stress for you. Is it something they do or some way they speak to you? What about them or the relationship makes it feel tricky?

After you figure out the source of the distress, you can establish boundaries to protect yourself and minimize the negative effect. I like to think of it as a tricky person game plan. For example, you might decide that when you see this person, you will limit your interaction (physical boundary), shift topics (mental boundary), or politely disengage (emotional boundary). These are ways of taking control and focusing on what you can manage so that you feel more empowered when dealing with tricky people.

If the relationship is optional, or no longer serves you, then do your best to eliminate any unnecessary time or interaction with the person, but if the relationship is unavoidable, you will need to set boundaries and find a way to physically, mentally, or emotionally detach from the dynamic while staying civil. Most of the time this comes up with family members, who are harder to avoid or eliminate from your life.

Clients often tell me that when they have to see someone that upsets them, they struggle to interact without getting triggered. I tell them that you can interact with these people in a detached but civil and respectful way that does not provoke conflict. Intentionally staying a little detached (emotionally guarded) helps you feel that you are not more emotionally vulnerable than you are comfortable with. I tell my clients to treat these people like the cashier at the grocery store: you can be nice and say hi and have a respectful interaction without having to feel vulnerable, defensive, or exposed.

Often it's hard to deal with tricky people because you may not understand why they cause you distress. You may also feel that you need something from them. When you need something (money, time, support, approval) from someone else, you feel vulnerable, and you don't feel as confident in being able to detach. However, by shifting your focus away from what you can't control and towards what you can control (amount of time together, topic of conversation, how much vulnerability you allow yourself), you will feel less anxious.

To reiterate some tactics to navigate challenging relationships:
1. Define who the tricky people are and what they do to affect you.
2. Set boundaries to protect your energy and help you detach.

3. Take control of your actions and reactions so you can focus on what you can manage and feel less anxious.
4. Determine whether the relationship is unavoidable or optional. If it's optional, opt out.
5. Work on your own emotional detachment by finding ways to avoid needing anything from the person. Stay civil and keep the peace if you can.
6. Lastly, if you need to walk away or set more extreme boundaries in unavoidable relationships, you must make yourself a priority and find a way to preserve your own well-being. This may be one of the hardest things you ever have to do, but when you say no to someone else, it's because you are saying yes to yourself.

Cultivating Strong Networks

Hillary Clinton popularized the phrase, "It takes a village" when she used it as the title for her book. Of course, this term predates her. It has been used in many cultures to refer to the idea that one person alone cannot raise a child: it takes a group of supportive people. I like to think that you also need a village to be an accomplished woman.

Although I made great friends in college, it wasn't until I became a mother that I joined a whole community of women that were all navigating the same problems. There is a vulnerability in being a mother (or being responsible for someone else) and it is a gift to have someone to support you when you need them. Community is something I've become grateful for. By being a part of the motherhood club, I've learned to deeply appreciate my relationships with other women.

I'm not saying that you have to be a mother to connect with other women: growing up, I watched many women around me connect deeply with other women. But when I became a mother, I learned to cultivate and appreciate my female relationships in a much different way.

I've also had many conversations with women who have struggled to deeply bond with other women. I think this is primarily because a woman's way of processing and expressing her emotions is multifaceted and to some degree unpredictable. It's valuable to learn about your own thoughts, feelings, and needs, so you can share them in your relationships and experience deeper connections. Remember my FRIENDS framework from earlier.

Your personal network is crucial for making you feel safe and enthusiastic about pursuing your ambitions. Think of it like an extended secure base that promotes your confidence and desire to explore and try new things.

As social creatures, we need to feel connected to other people and feel that we belong within a group. Your group can take the form of your family, a group, club, community, or simply several people you feel connected to and can rely on in various circumstances.

It's important to build up your personal network and have many different people you support and feel supported by. You've heard the saying, "Don't put all of your eggs in one basket." I like to think of eggs as friends or people in your network. I always encourage my kids to put their eggs in many baskets, and I encourage you to do the same. It's wonderful to have a best friend, but it is important to avoid relying solely on one person and better to know you have a network of people that you can turn to for community and support.

In the same regard, it is hard to get everything you need physically, emotionally, or psychologically from your spouse or partner. For those of you in heterosexual relationships, there are some things that guys just don't get and can't understand. That is why having female friends provides a totally different kind of support.

I've worked with many couples whose source of conflict is that there are things the wife wants and needs from her husband that he just can't give her—not because he won't, but because he can't. It's OK, and actually healthy, to get support and camaraderie outside of your relationship (just to be clear, I'm not suggesting you have an affair). In fact, it's better not to depend solely on your partner for all forms of support, because that is a lot of pressure and often leads to stress and frustration. Appreciate the limitations of your relationship, and take the initiative to seek friendships that fill in where you partner cannot.

It's better not to depend solely on your partner for all forms of support.

Cultivating Your Professional Network

Your professional network is a source of career advancement, mentorship, and other growth opportunities. Much of building this network consists of finding ways to show people what you have to offer and seek out opportunities for collaboration.

Connections with people with a range of professional perspectives and skills enable you to form a community for collaboration. You may decide to pursue a particular profession and may one day need guidance and support from someone in the same field. You might also be able to offer opportunities or partner up with people in your professional network.

You can identify and strengthen professional relationships in several ways. You can maintain connections with former colleagues and mentors by staying in touch, reaching out to check in, or even sending regular updates to keep the connection going. You never know whether reaching out to a former boss for advice or reconnecting with a former colleague who works at a company you admire might open unexpected doors.

You can also build new relationships with people you want to learn from, or you can find opportunities for mutual support. Introducing yourself by offering value is a great way to start a professional relationship based on shared goals and complementary skills.

It can be helpful to invest in your professional community or involve yourself in a professional organization. Networking events, conferences, or even online groups give you a chance to introduce yourself and make new contacts in your field or in a complementary field.

As a relationship and intimacy therapist, I often go to conferences for organizations, such as family law or ob-gyn, that don't directly relate to my services, although their clients could benefit from them. When I make contacts there, we can refer clients to one another as well as learning from one another. You can also provide value by introducing people who can benefit from knowing each other, which helps to build your professional network too.

Another great way to build your professional network is to offer value in the form of a presentation or workshop. You could donate your services to your community or your children's school, so people get to know you and what you have to offer. When I was starting out with my private practice, I would donate workshops to the annual school fundraiser, which gave me an opportunity to build my network.

Summary

At the end of the day, it's the people in your life who shape how supported, confident, and fulfilled you feel. The relationships you choose to nurture, whether they are personal or professional, have the power to uplift you, help you grow, and remind you that you don't have to do life alone. When you invest in meaningful connection, practice healthy boundaries, and surround yourself with people who truly see and support you, everything else gets easier.

Again, remember my FRIENDS framework: these are the ingredients for deeper, more authentic relationships. And don't forget that it's OK (and necessary) to set boundaries that protect your energy and allow you to show up as your best self. Not every relationship will be easy: some are tricky and will challenge you, but the more confident you become in navigating those dynamics, the more empowered you'll feel.

You deserve relationships that feel safe, reciprocal, and energizing. You deserve to be supported, to be seen, and to grow in the presence of people who bring out the best in you. Whether you're building your village or setting firmer fences, never underestimate the impact your relationships have on your overall well-being and success. Choose them wisely, nurture them intentionally, and don't be afraid to walk away from what no longer serves you. You are worth it.

Step Seven
Build and Strengthen Relationships that Matter and Protect Yourself with Good Boundaries

Action Plan and Exercises

Go get your journal, notebook, or guide, that favorite pen and a cup of tea. It's time to reflect on all that you've learned in this chapter.

EXERCISE ONE: USE THE FRIENDS FRAMEWORK

Choose one meaningful relationship in your life (friendship, romantic, or professional). Using the FRIENDS acronym, write down one thing you're already doing well for each letter and one thing you could improve.

For example:

F (fostering trust). I've been vulnerable about my anxiety, but I could be more consistent about checking in.

R. I respect her time, but I tend to push my needs down. I need to communicate them more clearly.

Keep going with the rest: -IENDS.

I.
E.
N.
D.
S.

EXERCISE TWO: USING THE BOLD METHOD

This exercise will help you practice setting a boundary for greater clarity and confidence.

Think of a real situation where you've wanted to say no or protect your time but have struggled. Write a boundary statement using the BOLD method:

Be clear.
Openly communicate.
Listen for response.
Defend your boundary in a kindly way.

For example, "I need quiet time after 8 p.m., so I won't be responding to texts or calls. I hope you understand."

EXERCISE THREE: A GAME PLAN FOR TRICKY PEOPLE

This exercise will help you feel more empowered when you are anticipating dealing with a tricky person. Knowing in advance how you will respond gives a feeling of control and makes you less anxious.

Identify one tricky person in your life. Answer the following questions:

1. What triggers me about them?
2. Is this relationship optional or unavoidable?
3. What boundaries do I need to set (physical, mental, emotional)?
4. What will my action plan be when I interact with them?

EXERCISE FOUR: CULTIVATING NETWORKS

This exercise will help you identify the important people in your relationship networks and determine how to strengthen those relationships. Draw two circles: one for your *personal network*, one for your *professional network*.

Inside each circle, list five to ten people who play (or could play) supportive roles.

Then write down one action you could take to strengthen or show appreciation for each relationship, such as a call, a thank you, a plan to spend time together, or offering support.

8

You Matter: Prioritize Your Health and Well-Being

DECADES OF LEARNING HOW to take care of my body and discovering exactly what I need to feel alert and strong have made me realize that if I don't have physical health and mental well-being, I just can't function at my best. I've come to appreciate the fact that your health is the foundation for everything else. Without health and energy, you can't show up physically, mentally, or emotionally.

In the fall of 2023, I had an experience that made me realize that no matter how good you are at setting goals, being proactive with your time, and investing in your relationships, an unexpected health crisis could derail your whole life.

It was about 2 a.m. when I woke up suddenly with a sharp pain in my back. It felt as if someone was stabbing me. No matter what position I moved to, I couldn't escape the discomfort. I tried to sleep. I lay there, evaluating what I could have done to injure myself, but I remained baffled.

The evening before, my husband and I had taken our youngest trick-or-treating for Halloween, and strolling through the neighborhood had been pleasant and uneventful. I hadn't fallen or hurt myself, so I couldn't trace a source of my pain. Regardless, I convinced myself that I had tweaked something in my back and needed to see a chiropractor. As soon as the morning came, I called and managed to get in to see him.

It was more pain than I'd ever experienced (and to give you an idea, I've been through three natural childbirths with no painkillers, so I'm no stranger to pain). This was unlike anything I'd felt before. The treatment with my chiropractor did nothing to alleviate the pain, and that day I had to drive to San Diego (a two-hour drive for me) to do a three-day speaker training with my father. It was not an option for me to cancel, since we had twelve people who had flown in from all over the world, and my dad was depending on me to share the responsibility of facilitating the training. I knew I'd have to find a way to show up.

My father has dealt with all kinds of health issues and has always willed himself through each ailment despite the toll it takes on his body. Once he did a seminar in London while hooked up to a pump delivering chemotherapy for his throat cancer. Another time we traveled together to South Korea and Shanghai where he led seminars for 10,000 people while in a wheelchair because his artificial hip had shattered and he couldn't walk. I'm not saying he is a good role model of self-care, but he certainly portrayed one approach to dealing with physical health issues.

So I did my best to emulate his "mind over matter" approach and despite being in agony (and fortunately on painkillers) I was able to get through the training without disappointing the participants, who seemed pleased with the value and had no idea that I was dying in pain.

I got home on Sunday. The next morning, I was sent for an MRI, which showed that somehow I had ruptured a disk in my neck, and it was squeezing the nerve to my left arm. While I had no idea what caused it, at least I knew there was a reason for my pain. After two attempts at spinal steroid injections to reduce the pressure and relieve the pain, I was sent to a spinal surgeon and was told my only option if I wanted to preserve the function of my arm was a disk replacement.

I had the surgery and have fortunately made a full recovery. I know that I'm lucky and not everyone goes through something like this with a success story, but beyond my physical recovery, I've come to realize the impact my health has on everything.

It was a month between that first night when I woke up in pain and the day I finally got the surgery and found relief. During that time, I struggled to show up for my clients, take care of myself, connect with my children, complete most tasks, and be a partner to my husband. In the meantime, my dysfunctional physical body distracted me from functioning in almost every way. For me, it was a physical injury that hijacked me from my life, but for some people, a mental health crisis or being burned out from stress can have the same impact.

Women are notorious for putting their needs second and overextending themselves for the needs of others. We defer our physical health and fitness, consider self-care optional, and overestimate how much stress we can handle. We also have the unique struggle of having to go through life performing at our best while navigating the impact of rapidly changing hormones through pregnancies, childbirth, perimenopause, and menopause. Not to mention the monthly hormonal shifts throughout our childbearing years.

Women are notorious for putting their needs second.

There are many factors to consider, but if you want to show up as the best version of yourself, you must take care of your body, protect your mental health, and find ways to manage your stress.

Your Health Is the Foundation

Your health really is the foundation for how you function in your life. You need to have physical health in order to move, take action, and get things done. It's also about energy: you need to have energy and vitality in order to use your body. It's not just about being able to do something, but also about having the stamina to keep up with the people in your life.

Your mental health plays a big role too. It affects your ability to focus and be present at home, at work, and anywhere you have responsibilities. It influences how well you manage your life and relationships. High stress levels drain you of physical health and take a toll on your mental health and well-being. That is why if you want to fortify the foundation of your health, you also need to learn how to manage stress.

In this chapter, you are going to learn how to prioritize your health and well-being with practical tools and exercises that will teach you how to protect your energy and boost your vitality. We will explore the impact of stress on your body and your relationships, learn how to manage your responsibilities to reduce stress, and implement simple techniques that allow you to process stress.

Women face many obstacles as we move through life, so we will also address those challenges and explore solutions so that you will feel more empowered to take care of your well-being

Finally, we are going to talk about ways to make your health a priority without compromising your many roles and responsibilities. Although it is often hard for women to take time away from others to invest in themselves, I want to show you how to do so without feeling guilty.

The Consequences of Neglect

When your mind and body are depleted, it's hard to be present, joyful, or even functional. When you are stressed out or not feeling well, you will find yourself more reactive, forgetful, and overwhelmed. If you are not healthy, you just can't do what you are truly capable of.

Your health is based on your energy: if you run out of energy, your battery will die, and you won't be able to engage. You always have to be aware of how much energy is depleted (which happens in many ways) and when you need to charge your battery.

If you neglect your health, don't recharge your battery, and don't take care of yourself, you will experience burnout, resent people you love, and end up suffering from a weak immune system and experiencing frequent illness. I'm always hearing excuses from women about how they don't have enough time to exercise or get enough sleep. They feel it's selfish to take care of themselves, or they defer their own needs and claim they "will do it later." In reality, if you don't take care of yourself and end up getting sick or suffer some other strain to your body or mental health, you will not be able to take care of anyone else. Put the oxygen mask on yourself first before you put it on someone else.

Benefits to Protecting Your Health

Protecting your health and managing stress will transform how you experience your life. You will have more energy, more stamina, a greater sex drive, and more enthusiasm for activities. Exercise is essential, especially as you age, and the benefits from maintaining a strong body and a healthy cardiovascular system are crucial to protecting your vitality and preventing injury. It is especially important for women in their late thirties and beyond to do strength training so they can protect their bones as they age.

Your body is the vehicle you use to engage in life. When you take care of it with rest, hydration, and a healthy lifestyle, you will benefit from being able to do everything you want—travel, dance, play with your kids, and go on adventures with your partner.

When you take care of your mental health and manage stress, you experience clarity and focus in executing tasks and pursuing your ambitions. Less stress means you are more present with the people you care about and more available for your family and friends. Not to mention the benefit of feeling calm, present, and fulfilled on a daily basis.

Easy, Practical Shifts to Protect Your Health

You've heard me talk about the importance of being proactive in your choices. Your health depends on being proactive. Nonetheless, taking care of your health does not mean that you need to totally overhaul your life: you just need to make small shifts that honor your mind and body. For example, my client Jasmine decided she would start eating her lunch sitting down at a table instead of standing while cleaning the kitchen. That one small shift gave her a midday reset that boosted her productivity for the rest of the day.

Another small shift you can make is setting a bedtime for yourself and sticking to it. Sleep research shows that when you go to bed and wake up at the same time every day (or at least within a one-hour time range), your body is more effective at physically and mentally rejuvenating while you sleep. Getting into a good circadian rhythm (sleep/wake cycle) has also been shown to boost your immune system and enhance your overall mood.

Another example is Alyssa, who started taking two short breaks from her office job to go outside and walk around the block. She was amazed to feel how much less depleted she was at the end of the day. Being outside, even for a short time, made her feel energized and enthusiastic for the rest of the day. I also know several moms who have adopted the habit of dropping their kids off at school and doing a daily walk before starting the day. If that doesn't work for you, you could also start taking a short walk after dinner in the evening. Moving your body, even a little, is good for your health and your mood.

When it comes to your mental health, nothing can give you a mental recharge like setting boundaries with your phone. I love to suggest that people set up a "charging station" in the kitchen: at certain times, they plug in their phones in and leave them in the charger. You can come back to check at any point, but at least the phone is not with you constantly. Setting boundaries around checking your emails is another great way to give your mental stress a break. Leaving your phone out of the bedroom will also improve your sleep and your intimacy with your partner (of course, they need to leave their phone out as well).

Nothing can give you a mental recharge like setting boundaries with your phone.

Setting Boundaries to Protect Your Health

Since your energy is directly linked to your health, I like to set boundaries in order to manage energy. You only have so much energy (emotional, mental, physical) before you burn out and your battery dies.

It's essential to determine what drains your battery and what charges it. For example, if you are an extraverted person, you probably love being around people and find it energizing. But if you are an introverted person, being around a lot of people will most likely use up a lot of energy and drain your battery.

You need to know how groups of people affect you when you are making social or work commitments. On an emotional level, certain subjects or experiences may be much harder for you than others and might drain your battery. As we've seen in the previous chapter, specific people can also drain your battery. You might have to limit your exposure to them. The same can be said about different physical or mental activities. Some will take more out of you than others. It's good to know your limits.

It's helpful to know what you can do to charge your battery, so you can set boundaries and make sure you get what you need. Setting boundaries is partly about knowing which people, relationships, and experiences can give you energy. You may feel rejuvenated by rigorous activity, or you might feel better taking time quietly by yourself. Think about what you can do to charge your battery. If you don't know, later in the chapter I will provide a great drain/charge chart that will help you.

People also demonstrate a range of intensity, which I like to refer to as a person's volume. If your energy and intensity is low or calm, your volume is low. If you have intense energy or are more active, you have a higher volume. Your volume also fluctuates depending on the circumstances. It's important to be aware of the kind of energy you give off as well as noticing the kind of energy people around you give off. When you operate at a low volume, interacting with someone who has high volume can feel intense or overwhelming. If you have high volume, it helps to be aware that your intense energy can overwhelm others and make it harder for them to express themselves with you. In relationships, you need to "tune" or match your volume with the other person so that you can communicate more effectively.

These are boundaries that you can set with others: You can ask them to lower their volume or match your intensity. (This is probably easier to introduce to your family and friends.) You can say something like, "Wow, you are really excited or passionate about this. I need you to slow down so I can process what you are saying." Or you can lower or soften your voice to influence the way they are communicating and show them how to lower their volume. If you are intense, practice being aware of how you match or don't match with people around you. It's important to make space for others in the conversation.

Tracking your volume and the volume of those around you will help you manage stress. Intense people are more stimulating to your nervous system: daily interactions with them can affect your stress levels. You can only take so much stimulation, whether it's environmental or from other people, before it affects your nervous system. We will talk more about how your daily interactions affect stress in the next section.

Let's Talk about Stress

Stress isn't just a feeling; it's a full-body experience. It affects how you think, how you feel, and how you behave. We need stress to motivate us to act, but too much stress can influence memory, focus, digestion, and even how you relate to others.

In a neutral state, when you are alert and present, your mind and body react in a certain way. You will naturally be drawn towards the things that you have a positive association with, and you will reject or move away from things with which you have negative associations. For example, if you enjoy interacting with an employee at your local coffee shop, you will look forward to the morning exchange, whereas if you hate sitting in traffic, you will dread the drive home. Positive anticipation leads to enthusiastic action, whereas negative anticipation leads to hesitant and reserved action.

Throughout the day, you accumulate more and more stimulation from the people you interact with and the environment you navigate. As a result, your stress level builds. You have less tolerance for additional stressors, and your response to people and additional stress changes. In this state of higher stress, you will naturally reject and move away from anything with which you have a negative association, but unfortunately you will also move away from things that you normally embrace and enjoy.

Say it's the end of the day, and you are organizing dinner. Your husband or child comes up wanting a hug or excited to tell you something. You might snap at them and tell them it's not a good time. Normally you would welcome the hug and be curious to hear all about what they wanted to share. That's because as your stress level builds, your tolerance for any additional stimulation, like talking, touching, or engaging, goes down. Eventually you have no room for anything else. Understanding this fact about stress is important for managing your responses and relating well with your loved ones.

On the flip side, when you are very relaxed and have had time to recharge your battery and decompress from the stress of the day, you will naturally show positive anticipation and embrace enthusiastic action towards the things you like. In a relaxed mind-body state, you will also be much more open-minded and curious to explore and engage with things that you are normally reluctant to approach.

In a relaxed mind-body state, you will be much more open-minded and curious to explore.

When you are relaxed, you are more open-minded and receptive. When you are stressed out and overstimulated, you are likely to reject. This is good to know so you can show up relaxed and receptive when you need to be.

There are plenty of tools you can use to lower your stress level throughout the day. I will describe some of these in the exercises at the end of the chapter.

Stress and Intimacy

Being relaxed and receptive is particularly important when it comes to sexual desire, pleasure, and intimacy. In general, sexual desire for men is very spontaneous. A man can be going through his day and suddenly feel the urge to have sex. He could be watching a football game and notice a surge of desire for no particular reason. This is also why men are frequently able to go from the chaos of dinner and putting kids to bed to walking into the bedroom and immediately being ready for intimacy. Their desire is spontaneous. Typically, it starts with an urge in the body, followed by a mental awareness and acceptance of the desire.

Women are different. In general (yes, there are exceptions) they need to convince their minds to give their bodies permission to experience desire and arousal. Women tend to have responsive desire: when stimulated by a gentle touch, a loving comment, an erotic image, they can decide in their minds if it's OK for their body to respond.

Let me tell you: a woman's biggest obstacle to intimacy is her mind. We are constantly telling ourselves that it's the wrong time or the wrong place, or maybe our partner did something that made us mad, and we haven't yet forgiven them. However, if you can find a way to decompress from stress and relax your body, it is much easier to be receptive to intimacy and desire. For my couples, I often suggest setting aside time for some kind of relaxing and connecting activity so that both people can show up and feel relaxed together before intimacy is introduced. For example, you could take a walk together, sit down for a glass of wine or a cup of tea, take a shower or bath together, or anything else that feels relaxing and lets you ease into intimacy.

A Woman's biggest obstacle to intimacy is her mind.

Create a Stress Reduction Ritual

A dedicated ritual that helps you decompress from stress is one of the most valuable things you can create for yourself. To do this, it's helpful to first map out when and where you feel the most stress. You might need to spend a week tracking your ups and downs so you can discover the pattern. At what time of the day do you find yourself the most overwhelmed and stressed out? Do you feel it in your body? For me, stress shows up as a knotted stomach, a fuzzy headache, or tight shoulders. Connecting to the location of the stress in your body helps you decide the best decompression ritual for the occasion. You can also try to determine the root of the stress and explore if there was time pressure, a lack of support, or any guilt associated with how you were spending your time and energy.

Next, determine what kind of ritual would help you get into your body and feel more relaxed. There are many things you can do. You don't need to commit to an hour-long yoga session: your ritual could be as short as five minutes. You could do something like "box breathing," where you inhale for four seconds, hold for four seconds, and exhale for four seconds. You do this four times: it helps you calm your nervous system. You could also turn on your favorite song and dance to it. Or a better ritual for you may be getting a coffee or a tea and sitting down to journal for a couple of minutes (or an hour if you want). I had one client who would sit down with her planner and write out all of her tasks and responsibilities for the next day, which would free her of pent-up stress and anticipation.

Of course, you could do that one-hour yoga class or some kind of rigorous exercise. Sometimes when I feel frustrated, I love to run and sweat. It really depends on what works best for you.

You could also come up with different rituals for the amount of time or the specific need you have. The important thing is proactively establishing some rituals to lean on when you need to boost your energy and focus or calm your body and relax. Just feeling more in control by having a tool will help you manage the stress of your day.

Summary

This chapter is deeply personal for me, because I've lived the truth that your health really is the foundation for everything else. No matter how well you plan, how motivated you are, or how committed you feel, if your physical or mental health takes a hit, everything else can fall apart. I shared my own personal story about my sudden health crisis because it reminds me that women, especially those of us balancing families, careers, and big ambitions, are quick to put ourselves last. We underestimate the toll of stress, overlook the signals from our bodies, and tell ourselves we'll rest or recover "later."

But if we're not taking care of our bodies or protecting our mental health, we can't show up for anyone else, not our partners, our kids, our clients, or ourselves. We must make our health a priority.

In this chapter, we talked about how burnout shows up, and your battery can die if you don't charge it. We explored how energy is essential to our health and a resource we must protect. We discussed the impact of neglecting our health on everything from engaging in our lives to functioning in work to how we show up in intimacy. We talked about some simple, practical ways to integrate small shifts that can dramatically improve how you feel and function, such as setting a phone boundary, creating a bedtime routine, or just getting outside for a walk. These small actions don't require overhauling your entire life, but they can make a big difference.

We also explored how stress is not just a feeling, but something that can affect your whole mind-body experience. Your level of stress affects your ability to focus on tasks, the way you relate to people, and how you show up in your relationships. It has a significant impact on your partnership and how you experience desire and intimacy. When you're stressed out, you're likely to reject even the good things. When you're relaxed, you're open, curious, and connected. That's not just about your experience with intimacy; it's about how you experience every area of your life.

Lastly, we talked about proactively creating decompression rituals that you can implement whenever you need them. Whether you need a boost or a way of calming your mind and body, you have the responsibility and the power to take care of yourself so you can show up for your work, your family, and yourself.

Step Eight
Prioritize Your Health and Well-Being

Action Plan and Exercises

Take a moment to think about all that we've covered in this chapter. Now go get your journal or guide and give yourself a couple of minutes to go through the following exercises and determine how you will make yourself a priority.

EXERCISE ONE:
REFLECTING ON WHAT YOUR HEALTH MEANS TO YOU

The purpose of this exercise is to get you to connect to how your health affects your life and see why it is so important to invest in protecting your health and managing stress. Take your journal or guide and answer the following questions:

1. How does your health influence the way you show up for your family, your work, and yourself?
2. What do you need more of in order to feel less stress and have better energy?
3. What can you do less of to improve your health?
4. What is one action you plan to take to improve your health?

EXERCISE TWO:
PROTECT YOUR ENERGY AND CHARGE YOUR BATTERY

Doing this exercise will help you set better boundaries based on your own energy awareness. Draw two columns (or use the table below). In the first column, call it the "drain" column, list everything you can think of that drains your energy. In the second column—call it the "charge" column—write a list of everything that fortifies you or gives you a boost of energy.

Next, reflect on your last seven days, and list people, activities, conversations, or settings under each column. Then, circle the top two or three "drainers" and identify a boundary you can set for each one to preserve your energy. Circle the top two or three "chargers" and determine how you can integrate those activities into the next week.

Drain	Charge

EXERCISE THREE: YOUR SLEEP RESET

This exercise is meant to bring your awareness to your sleep patterns and set a new sleep plan so you can feel more energy and mental clarity on a daily basis. You are going to:

1. Set a consistent bedtime and wake-up time (within a one-hour range) for seven days.

2. Document the last five things you do before you go to sleep (teeth brushing, water, TV).
3. Track your sleep quality, mood, and focus each day.
4. Leave your phone out of the bedroom and see how that affects your rest and relationships.
5. At the end of the week, name one thing you will commit to continuing in order to improve your sleep.

EXERCISE FOUR: MENTAL RECHARGE BREAKS

This exercise will help you integrate little ways to boost your focus and energy while reducing stress and without taking away from your responsibilities. Every day for the next week I want you to:

1. Schedule two ten-minute breaks during your day.
2. Choose from the following options, or come up with one yourself:
- Take a short walk outside.
- Try box breathing: four seconds in, four seconds hold, four seconds out. Do this four times.
- Listen to your favorite song (and dance if you want).
- Stretch or move your body.

Reflect at the end of the day and note if these breaks have changed your energy or focus.

EXERCISE FIVE: PHONE BOUNDARY CHALLENGE

This exercise will help you connect to the impact your phone has on your mental well-being and show how boundaries can bring you peace of mind, help reduce overstimulation at the end of day, and increase your presence. (This is a great family or couples activity.)

For one week:
1. Set up a phone charging station away from your bedroom and dining area.
2. Establish a cut-off time for checking emails or social media.
3. Journal or discuss with someone how you feel after three days.

EXERCISE SIX: PRACTICE RECEPTIVITY AND CONNECTION TIME

This is a great way to help you create a ritual that allows you to warm up to connecting with your partner, letting go of the stress of the day, and becoming more receptive to intimacy.

1. Schedule one evening (or day) with your partner for a "relax and connect" ritual, such as taking a walk, having a glass of wine, or taking a bath together. (There is no pressure for intimacy: this is just to relax and connect.)
2. Ask your partner what they experienced and share if you felt more open or connected. Also note whether you experienced greater desire for intimacy.

EXERCISE SEVEN: CREATE YOUR DECOMPRESSION RITUAL(S)

This exercise will help you identify a ritual you can create to enable you to go from feeling stressed to feeling calm and relaxed (or feeling stressed and distracted to being more present and focused). Using your journal or guidebook,

1. Briefly reflect on the day and notice when and where you felt the most stressed for three days.
2. Schedule a daily ritual that can help you decompress (examples: journaling, music, walking, breathing) and keep track of how you felt after the ritual.
3. Once you find a ritual you like, commit to trying it once a day for a week, even for just five minutes.

Chapter 9
Improve Your Relationship with Money and Become Financially Empowered

MONEY IS A TRICKY subject. As a couples therapist, I've learned that most conflicts in relationships revolve around money and sex. I will admit that at the beginning of my career, the idea of working with people to improve their relationship with money was daunting to me. I was no expert in money matters, and I wouldn't have said that I had the best relationship with money. But I've done a lot of work on myself around the subject, and I do appreciate how important it is to understand your feelings about it in order to improve that relationship and feel more financially empowered.

Most conflicts in relationships revolve around money and sex.

I spent the first six years of my life in Edmonton, Alberta, Canada. My family had a modest lifestyle, and I remember frequently eating spaghetti for dinner and taking walks around the neighborhood. We never talked that much about money, but once in a while my parents would take my brother and me to the Four Seasons Hotel for a "fancy" dinner, where we would practice our table etiquette so one day we would be prepared to "dine with the queen," as my mother would say. We would dress up and act like rich people (from my young perspective).

When I was seven, we moved to California, and everything changed. My father's business took off, and we moved into a giant house (in comparison to our cozy three-bedroom house in Canada). Money seemed to be a subject that my parents discussed a lot—never with us kids, but we would hear them talking about money, especially as it related to success and business. In fact, I got the message early on that money was private, and you don't ask people about it.

I was out to dinner with my family when I was about nine. After the waiter took our order, I looked up at him and innocently asked how much money he made. My father nearly died. He turned to me and said, "Christina, you never ask a person how much money they make; it's like asking them what color underwear they are wearing." I was shocked but got the message loud and clear: do not talk about money; do not ask questions.

Over the next decade, my dad traveled all the time, and in his absence we would do a lot of shopping (or so it seemed). My dad prided himself on being a provider, and I think that since he was gone so much, my mother wanted us to feel his hard work and devotion by compensating for his absence with toys and gifts. Both my parents had grown up poor and wanting. When the money started flowing, the idea that they could give their children a different experience was exciting. Their attitude toward money influenced how we related to it. It was great to be able to participate in classes and camps, have new clothes for school, and the latest trendy gadget, but all these gifts had an unexpected effect on me and my relationship with money.

I learned to associate money with love and took on the belief that if someone loves you, they buy you things; if you love someone, you buy them things. If someone stops buying you things or tells you that you can't have something, it has nothing to do with the practicality of a budget, but everything to do with them not loving you and you not being worth the cost.

I was financially supported by my parents when I was in school. Since they paid the credit card bill and the college tuition, I had no idea how to budget or handle money. In truth, I never kept track of my spending and had no concept of limitations or debt. My parents were private about money, and I knew not to ask. As far as I understood, they were supporting me and loving me through my credit card, and, boy, did I make sure I felt that love.

Fast forward to getting married. My parents had always said that they would support me until I got a job and could support myself or until I got married (not a good message for the financial empowerment of women, but a traditional view).

A month after our wedding, we got our first credit card bill. My poor husband nearly had a heart attack. He had grown up with a completely different relationship with money. His parents were frugal and outspoken about their financial situation. There was no shame or secrecy in talking about money. This was a shock to me, since I had grown up with the exact opposite view. Both of us came from similar financial backgrounds, but whereas in my family I learned very little about money that was practical, in his family he had learned the value of money and how to budget and invest from a young age.

We were actually a terrible combination when it came to money. He had learned that the goal was to save money, spend as little as possible, and reject luxuries. I had learned that love comes in the form of money and gifts, and the more you love, the more you give. Can you imagine how heartbroken I was when my husband didn't love me enough to "let me" spend as much money as I wanted? It was the source of years of conflict for us. In the end it was also a gift for both of us in that we found a healthy mix of spending and saving, but now we've been together twenty-seven years, and sometimes my "money script" still rears its ugly head.

I have learned to respect and appreciate money and to see it as a tool. I can't fully separate my emotional attachment to spending, but I've become more financially empowered. Starting my own private practice as a therapist and learning to set fees for my services taught me about the value of money and service. I'm still working on building my confidence when talking about money, negotiating rates, and selling my services, but I'm in a much better place than I once was. I've grown a lot and have learned how to value my effort as a mother without receiving a paycheck. But I would not be where I am if I hadn't first explored my relationship with money and how it affected my life.

Women, Worth, and the Meaning of Money

Money can be an especially emotional topic for women. Many of us weren't taught how to handle it; we just absorbed the stress, guilt, or silence around it. Whatever your experience has been, it has had an impact on how you value yourself and your efforts and what money means to you. Whether you work full-time or part-time or are a full-time mom running a household, your relationship with money is worth exploring.

One thing that motivated me to write this book was that I know there are many amazing women making contributions as mothers, as community members, or as sole entrepreneurs with their small businesses, yet they devalue themselves because of what they believe is the traditional definition of success: large paychecks and big promotions. No wonder so many stay-at-home moms struggle over feeling "successful" despite managing a household and raising children.

Many women devalue themselves because of what they believe is the traditional definition of success: large paychecks and big promotions.

We need to rewrite these outdated definitions, because financial success is much more than income. It's about how you use your money to support your freedom, your security, and your ability to live in alignment with your values. You can earn six figures, but if you are burned out and unaligned with your values, you won't feel successful.

Financial success is about having choices and being able to use money to facilitate those choices. It's about feeling confident in your money managing skills and having self-awareness about your emotional connection to money. It's about feeling empowered to notice your feelings and behavior about money and how they relate to your beliefs about self-trust, self-worth, or sense of deserving. That self-reflection empowers you to proactively respond in a way that feels good to you. In any relationship, the more you invest, the more rewarding it becomes. The same goes for money.

In this chapter, we are going to explore the psychology of money and learn practical skills for spending and saving. We will explore how women often have complicated relationships with money in terms of advocating for themselves, setting fees, and demanding what they are worth. They struggle to value themselves whether they receive a paycheck or not.

You will learn how to improve your relationship with money and discover what it means to you and how that affects the way you use it. You will develop practical skills around money management and budgeting. You will also learn how to have conversations around money and set financial goals for yourself personally and professionally in order to feel financially confident and empowered. Ultimately, I want you to understand how you currently relate to money and create the relationship with it that you desire.

Your Emotional Relationship with Money

Your emotional relationship with money has a powerful impact. By understanding your feelings about this subject, you become more empowered and can choose how to relate to it. You need self-awareness before you can change your behavior.

One major issue that holds women back from feeling fully accomplished is the sense of being out of control in regard to money. Women commonly desire to achieve financial independence so they will not feel beholden or controlled by anybody, whether it be to a boss, a spouse, or a parent. This is a major cause of anxiety and insecurity.

Psychologist Abraham Maslow established what he called the "hierarchy of needs," a theory of psychological health and well-being that is based on priorities. Maslow discovered that the most basic human desire is for security. We seek security before we can think clearly about anything else. Therefore, feeling that your money is controlled by someone else undermines your sense of security and can cause anxiety and stress. That's why it's important to feel empowered financially: so you can confidently pursue your goals and ambitions. There is also something very powerful about knowing you can provide for yourself in the present and the future. This is a major contributor to your self-esteem and your engagement in life.

The most basic human desire is for security.

Money can bring up feelings such as anger, fear, and guilt, as well as positive feelings like comfort and love. Those feelings deeply affect whether you spend or save or avoid money altogether. Think about it for yourself: how do you feel about money now? How in control of your finances do you feel? Control has to do with how much influence you feel you have with your money versus how much you believe other people control your access to it. Reflect on the emotion that comes up for you when you think about spending or saving money.

Here is an example: Tina gets anxious every time she gets her credit card statement and thinks about paying bills. She feels this way because when she was growing up, bills in her house were a source of stress and conflict, so naturally she learned to fear and often avoid her bills. To some degree, she does not feel in control of her spending and therefore fears the consequence of not budgeting properly.

Ideally, we would all see money as a tool, approach it from a practical place, and make logical decisions, but most people let their emotions influence their behavior. In my story, I told you about how money felt like love to me, so I justified my overspending because it made me feel good. But this didn't release me from paying my bills. Some of our parents grew up affected by financial scarcity or economic depression, and their fear about running out of money caused them anxiety and feeling out of control. Some reacted by turning into supersavers or even hoarders.

When money brings up negative feelings, the easiest thing to do is avoid it. If you are the kind of person who doesn't check your balance or want to talk about money, what negative feelings come up for you? I want you to face your fear.

Here is an exercise to get you started. Answer the following questions:

When I think about money, I feel _____

The message I learned about money was _____

I want to feel _____ about money

I feel in control of my money when _____

I feel out of control of my money when _____

Acknowledge what makes you feel in and out of control. You can allow a stack of unopened bills to pile up, or you can set regular financial check-ins to keep track of where you are and adjust your spending. Control builds confidence and eventually eliminates fear.

Uncovering your Money Script

The first time I heard of the money script was when I read the book *Mind over Money: Overcoming the Money Disorders That Threaten Our Financial Health*, by Brad and Ted Klontz. The idea is that we each have a "money script," a playbook that guides our thoughts, feelings, and behavior around this subject. We are introduced to these scripts as kids, and we continue our stories as we move through life. They shape the meaning we create around money as well as how we show up financially today. Whether we are overly giving, underearners, overspenders, or afraid to talk about money at all, we have subconscious beliefs from childhood that shape how we relate to this matter. Some common scripts are, "Money doesn't grow on trees," "There is never enough," or "Success equals income." We hear these ideas from our parents, and we absorb what we see them do. They model to us how we should react, think, and feel about money. Those beliefs still have an effect even when circumstances change.

My client Sarah grew up hearing her parents respond to things she wanted to spend money on by asking her, "Do you really need that?" or "Do you really need a second pair of those?" She got the message that there wasn't enough money and they "couldn't afford it." Now as a successful adult, she believes it's wrong to spend money on herself. Even though she has made millions of dollars, she still insists on shopping at thrift stores because she doesn't "need" new clothes.

A money script is a core belief system, so when you grow up with "not enough money" or as a "poor person" and then become rich, you may find yourself losing or mismanaging your money, because on a deeper level you still subscribe the idea that you are poor and can't afford what you want. As a result, you recreate that old reality despite the changed circumstances. The only way to break the pattern is to identify your money script and decide it no longer serves you. Work proactively to shift your attitude and behavior so that you can incorporate a new script whereby you are successful and capable of financial security despite your past.

A money script is a core belief system.

Here is another example, Marie grew up with wealth, and her father was very generous with money as long as she and her two brothers took his advice and made the choices he wanted them to make. He dictated whom she could be friends with and where she went to college. She never questioned him because she was afraid that if she did, he would stop supporting her, so she learned to cooperate and never ask for more, or she might lose everything.

When Marie grew up, she married a wealthy man and struggled for years to assert herself and have an opinion about money out of the fear that he too would use it to control her. Luckily, he was supportive. When she shared her fear, he helped her replace her money script with the idea that she could trust, speak up, and make choices for herself without financial consequences.

Many women grow up with the idea that talking about money is rude or inappropriate or is something men deal with. As a result, they struggle to set fees, negotiate job offers, or even talk to their husbands about money. This causes them to get into traditional relationships and step into the understanding, based on their own scripts, that the husband manages the money. As a result, they don't learn about their finances or participate in decisions around saving and spending. This causes them to feel out of control. It can lead to anxiety and a feeling of being beholden to someone. The other problem is that if something happens to the husband or the relationship doesn't work out, these women are at a disadvantage, because they don't have enough knowledge about their own money and can't make crucial decisions.

I've heard many horror stories of women who didn't take an interest in their finances; when the husband died, they had no idea where the money even was. In the case of my friend Joan, who let her husband manage their finances because she worked full-time at her own business, she was left to clean up the mess after getting divorced and finding out he had run up thousands of dollars of debt. I'm all about trusting your partner and assuming the best, but if you want to feel financially empowered—even as a full-time stay-at-home mom—please take an interest in your finances so you can make informed decisions. If your money script tells you that you shouldn't ask questions, maybe challenge that narrative: ask some questions and see how you feel.

While your money script has a huge influence on your behavior, the good news is that you can rewrite it. Your awareness is the first step to shifting beliefs that no longer serve you. Question why you do what you do. Think about your current money script: does it feel true to you, or does it no longer serve you? If it no longer serves you, take some time to reflect on what you do believe about money as well as how you would like to think, feel, and behave going forward. This is especially important if you have children, because they are learning from you and will repeat the money script you teach them. What beliefs do you want them to absorb? If you're married, ask you partner what they believe and see how you can proactively work together with money.

When Money Becomes Love

Many of us use money to express love, feel loved, or prove our worth. We spend on our kids instead of ourselves. We give gifts instead of asking for affection. We say yes to financial requests because saying no feels like rejection. But love and money are not the same thing. For many women, money is a stand-in for love, care, approval, or worth. This can lead to overspending, overgiving, and resentment.

As a huge supporter of love languages, I know that for some people, receiving a gift is not about the gift; it's about the fact that someone thought about them when they were apart; that makes them feel valued and important. But it becomes a problem when a person gives a gift or money to compensate for genuine, undivided attention or concern. Or when the gift is misinterpreted and causes resentment because it becomes expected rather than appreciated. Using money to substitute for emotional needs leads people to feel that gifts, spending, or earning are the only ways they are lovable. That creates unhealthy relationship dynamics and lowers self-esteem.

When I was a teenager, I would ask my dad for some money to go to the movies and get some food with my friends. He would always double what I asked for and told me that I should pay for them. He felt proud of his success and his ability to be generous with others. He would explain to me that when you are doing well in life, you should always take care of people who were not as fortunate. It's a beautiful idea and very kind and generous, but unfortunately, when I paid for my friends, they did not understand. They either felt insulted or took advantage of the fact that I would often cover the cost of our time together. I went through a period of not knowing if my friends were genuine or if they were just taking advantage of my generosity. It was painful to work through that. I was "loving" them in the way that I had received "love," and it did not have a positive effect.

Money as love also has to do with you. Many women connect their earning ability or financial achievement with their self-worth. They have a hard time feeling validated when they are not earning money, or "enough" money. I work with many clients to help them identify the value they bring to their families, friends, jobs, or community. It's always amazing to me how much women underestimate the importance of their care, efforts, and thoughtfulness to the people around them.

Many women connect their earning ability or financial achievement with their self-worth.

Love and money are not the same thing. You are lovable because of who you are, not because of what you give or earn. Untangling love from money allows us to build healthier relationships, with others and with ourselves.

Here is an exercise to explore your connection between love and money.

Reflect on where money might feel like love. Answer these questions:

1. I give when I really want _____
2. I feel most loved when _____
3. One way I'll give love without guilt or overspending is _____

When Money Becomes Control

Now let's talk about another aspect of money dynamics: when money is used to manipulate or control, especially in close relationships. It might be subtle, like guilt-tripping your spending, or direct, like not letting you access money. Sometimes control shows up when your relationship feels transactional: where you feel you need to earn your ability to spend money or do activities. As we've seen, there are many stories of women giving their partners responsibility for the finances and ending up in a bad situation because they were uninformed.

Teri is married, with three kids, and she is a full-time mom. Her husband works. They agreed at the beginning that she would stay home and take care of the kids while he was the primary earner. However, the kids are older now and Teri wants to work again, but her husband adamantly refuses to let her get a job: he wants her to be available when and if the kids need her. He is also reluctant to use any childcare, so Teri only gets a break briefly, while the kids at school. She knows she is in a toxic marriage and her freedom is limited, but she has no financial independence and no ability to support herself, so she stays.

Erin's partner insists on managing all the finances and gives her a weekly allowance, even though she works part-time and contributes to expenses. He claims that they should both contribute equally to the bills, even though he makes much more, which limits how much allowance she can have. He also makes her feel guilty when she does spend her allowance. She justifies this dynamic because he is earning more money and therefore, she believes, should have more control over spending.

Financial control issues don't only show up with partners. I see a lot of controlling dynamics in families between parents and children, even between parents and adult children. For example, Lily and her sister Melissa both moved to the city where their parents lived because the parents offered to buy them each a home if they lived nearby. Now Lily and Melissa both feel obligated to stay close although they want to move to other cities.

Another type of case is when parents support their adult children, who fail to launch or become fully capable of supporting themselves. Sometimes the intention is purely out of a sense of duty and responsibility for their children, but sometimes financially supporting them fosters dependency and makes it harder for them to be fully independent. These adults are beholden to their parents and feel obligated to do what they are asked or expected to do, even when it does not serve them. Here are some warning signs to look out for if you are feeling like you don't have control of your money, or someone might be using money as a source of control:

1. You don't have access to the household bank accounts.
2. You feel guilty every time you spend money, even on essentials like groceries.
3. Someone else uses your financial dependency to control your decisions.

If you relate, you can start to reclaim your autonomy by understanding your finances and taking the first step to more financial freedom and healthier boundaries. Determine to what degree you have financial autonomy. Do you have access to money? Can you make decisions without fear or anxiety? Is there an action you can take to feel more informed and in control of your finances?

Reclaim your autonomy by understanding your finances and taking the first step to more financial freedom and healthier boundaries.

Value Your Work, Paid or Not

There is much value in unpaid work. In fact, I'm willing to say that without the unpaid work of raising children, managing a household, and volunteering for the greater good, we would have a real problem. I recently read the book *The Wife Drought: Why Women Need Wives and Why Men Need Lives*, by Annabel Crabb. She talks about how a "wife" is not just a woman, it's a role, and that those fortunate enough to have a "wife" perform better at their jobs, go further in their careers, and achieve their goals faster. What a "wife" does—cooking, cleaning, managing the house, being on call for children, raising children, volunteering at school, driving—is not reflected in a paycheck. Yet women have a hard time appreciating that their time, their labor, and their emotional effort all have tremendous value; they are essential. You are contributing whether you bring in income or are running the home.

This can be part of an identity shift for women who step back from the traditional workforce and don't know how to justify or talk about their efforts. Think about how often when you are in a social situation, people will ask you what you do. For those who have stepped back to take care of children, this can be a particularly hard question, and one that can make them feel invisible. On the flip side for women who are full time mothers they often feel judged for not also having a paid job.

I often work with couples around money issues. We talk about how each partner contributes, and that contribution is not limited to dollars. It is very emotional to feel dependent on a partner, especially if you've been independent but have now chosen to work less or raise kids. For many couples, this brings up fear and anxiety. Often the earning partner needs to reinforce the value contributed by the nonearning partner.

For example, Mark bought a house for him and his wife, Julie, from savings he had built up over the years. While Julie could not contribute financially, she spent time furnishing and decorating the house, making it a home. Mark could not have done that, and he was grateful that she created such a warm, inviting place to live. It was hard for Julie to accept that she was not contributing financially, but she eventually saw that she brought value to their home in a different way.

Remember, your time and energy have value. Take an inventory of your invisible labor and validate for yourself how much value you offer. Think about all the unpaid or unrecognized labor you do in a week. This includes emotional support, household chores, scheduling, and caring for children.

Now assign a realistic hourly rate to each chore. If you had to hire someone to do these tasks, how much would you have to pay? You will see that everything you do has value.

Self-Worth: Ask for What You Deserve

Given many relationship dynamics, societal messages, and learned behaviors, it's no wonder many women undervalue themselves. They struggle to ask for raises, set fair rates, and confidently state their worth. For many women, this struggle has a lot to do with their own self-worth and believing that they are worthy or that the value they provide should be paid for.

You have to believe in your own value before anyone else will. The more you value yourself and the work you do, the more others will value it. When you charge for your time others value your time differently. It makes me think of the story of Evian mineral water. At first, the brand was only charging $1 for a bottle. Then they decided to increase the price to $3 per bottle. As soon as they did, people's perception of the water changed. They began to believe it was special: since it was more expensive, it must be of higher value.

You have to believe in your own value before anyone else will.

I found this idea to be true in the service industry as well, whether I'm charging therapy clients, selling coaching packages, or setting a speaking rate. When you charge an amount that is at the higher end of the typical range for your service, people are more invested and take it more seriously. If you charge too little or give it away for free, people are less committed and don't take it seriously. The challenge is having the confidence to set the rate and ask for it.

One way to gain the confidence to ask for money is to start thinking about the value you offer. How do you serve others? What result do you help people achieve? In business, we talk about "offers." You *offer* someone a transformation or a result, and then you ask them to pay for it. It's not about the process of achieving the result, but the actual result that has value.

I was just at a networking event when one participant got up and offered a closet edit to help professional women put together outfits that made them look and feel empowered and confident. The woman who uses this service will go from feeling unattractive or not put together to feeling attractive and confident. The confidence she will feel will allow her to sell her own products and services more effectively, and her business will grow. That has a lot of value: the woman's investment in her own style will earn her more money. How much would you pay to feel more confident?

I love the concept that the more you serve, the more you deserve. In other words, the more value you provide, the more money you should earn. If you believe you are worthy and provide value, you can work towards the financial goals you set for yourself.

In my group trainings, people often say they feel guilty about wanting to earn a lot of money. As we explore people's feelings and money scripts, I often hear of money being associated with evil or bad intentions. However, the deeper we dig and the more we explore, the more we come to conclude that earning more money is good, because it enables you to help more people. You can grow your business and serve more people, so you can donate your money to causes you care about and buy freedom and time to do what matters most to you.

Another way to gain confidence and ask for what you're worth goes back to setting boundaries. Start saying no to free work: when people ask for your help, value your time and ask for compensation. The more you value your time, the more others will as well. Get into the habit of saying things like, "I provide this value, and the results I get are . . . so here is what I charge for my time . . ." If you are asked to do something that achieves results for others, practice saying things like, "I would be happy to help you with that, but before we get started, I'd like to talk about compensation." It's amazing to watch what happens when you start asking for compensation. Many women are reluctant to ask for money or raise their rates, but as soon as they do, they get more clients and earn more money. I have found this to be true for myself, my clients, and many of my friends.

Start saying no to free work.

Talking about Money with Confidence

Since most people feel emotional around money, conversations about it can be loaded. Start by breaking the taboo: normalize money conversations by having them with the people in your life, such as partners, children, friends, coworkers, and even your boss. The more you practice the casual money conversation, the easier it becomes to have the harder money conversations.

This was really hard for my client Lauren, but after years of avoiding money conversations with her family, she told her parents that she wanted to be responsible for her own financial planning and asked for access to all her account information. Surprisingly to her, they were proud of her taking the initiative and very supportive of her taking over. Lauren had started by having conversations with her female friends about how they budgeted and managed their money. Those conversations made her feel more comfortable with the subject and gave her the confidence to talk to her parents.

I think it's great for couples to have weekly money conversations. You start by having money check-ins with your partner. Come from a productive place, without judgment and with the intention of working as a team towards joint goals. Ideally you should both collaborate to make sure each of you gets your needs met. Learn to communicate clearly and calmly so you can assert yourself without being aggressive or defensive. You can say things like, "This is what I need; how can we make that work?" or "Let's discuss the budget together and make sure we are on the same page." Financial intimacy strengthens relationships, and not just romantic relationships. Transparency and honesty about money leads to deeper trust and partnership all around.

Practical Financial Skills

Practical financial skills have to do with budgeting, spending, and saving money. It starts with knowing your numbers: how much is coming in, how much is going out, and where it is all going. When you understand cash flow, you can set up a budget and practice keeping track and checking your daily balance. With that awareness, you can make smarter choices. You can stop feeling that money is something you don't have control of.

From here, you can build your financial literacy. Basic budgeting starts by determining what you want or need to spend on to support yourself. Then you determine how much you can spend and how much you need to save in order to cover your expenses.

In general, you never want to spend more money than you are earning, because that will lead to debt. Getting into the habit of saving a portion of your income will come in handy later, when you need to make a big purchase or aren't earning as much. It also gives you a great sense of security to know you have money saved up if you ever need it. Most people try save a little bit each month, even if it's only $25 that automatically goes into savings for an emergency fund. You will feel more secure and in control if you manage to build up a backup fund.

Investing money is a great idea. I recently spoke with Kerry, a financial advisor, who explained that anyone can invest at any level. It allows you to benefit from compounding, meaning that interest on your money earns you a return. The longer your money compounds, the more it makes. Kerry also observes that money is just like health: when you decide to improve it and you start taking the steps, say to lose weight, have better energy, and sleep more soundly, you put your focus there, and that gets you results. When you shift your focus to financial health, you become more mindful of your spending and more proactive with your saving and investing. It starts with making money a priority and giving it more of your attention.

All you have to do is take small, consistent actions that move you forward. That might mean setting up automated savings, using a spending tracker, or simply checking in with your finances once a week. These little steps compound over time, leading you to financial empowerment. Remember, you don't need to be perfect, but you do need to be present and proactive. That's how you build financial confidence.

All you have to do is take small, consistent actions that move you forward.

Empowering Financial Goals

It's important to motivate yourself with a financial goal that is measurable and time-bound. That starts with gaining clarity on your situation, then taking action. For example, your goal can be saving $5,000 by December. That goal and that action are clearly established.

Setting financial goals is not a just a way of managing money; it's a mindset about your finances. It's about taking ownership of your financial situation. The more you set goals and work towards them, the more in control you will feel and the more your relationship with money will improve.

For example, Michelle dreamed of writing a book but felt she would never find the time to take on the project. She decided she needed to take time off work in order to dedicate herself to writing. She set a goal of saving $10,000. With a plan, over two years she was able to put the money aside and have the funds to support her while she took a sabbatical from her job.

Alisha is another example of someone who took control of her financial situation. After years of avoiding her bank balance and hating her bills, she decided to create a five-year plan to pay off her student loans. She started by making one extra payment every three months. Alisha was amazed at how much more confident she felt financially just by taking action towards something she had feared and avoided. She realized that feeling empowered was not just about having money: it's about believing in yourself and your ability to handle what comes your way.

Summary

As we wrap up this chapter, I want to remind you that your relationship with money is just that: a relationship. Like in any relationship, when you are proactive, aware, intentional, and invested, it gets better. You are not stuck with the old money scripts you absorbed or the habits you learned growing up. You have the power to rewrite your script and shift the way you think, feel, and act around money. When you start to understand your emotions, set boundaries, value your contributions, and build practical skills, you move from feeling out of control to feeling empowered.

Money isn't about proving your worth: it's about asking for what you are worth, creating choices, and building freedom. You have the power to set financial goals that allow you to live in alignment with what matters most to you. Every small step you take strengthens your confidence and your future. You are capable of creating a healthy, empowered relationship with money, and you deserve to feel that security, confidence, and freedom.

Step Nine
Improve your relationship with money and take action towards feeling financially empowered.

Action Plan and Exercises

Its time to get your journal or The Accomplished Woman's Guide, your favorite pen, a cup of tea or coffee and find a peaceful place to reflect for a couple minutes.

EXERCISE ONE: DEFINE WHAT FINANCIAL SUCCESS MEANS TO YOU

The purpose of this exercise is to get you to connect with what financial success looks like for *you*—not society, not your parents, not your friends. I want you to connect with what it means to be financially successful and why that is important to you. In your journal or notebook, answer the following questions.

1. What do you truly value?
2. How would it feel to be financially successful on your own terms?
3. What would your life look like if money were in alignment with your worth?

Then write a paragraph stating what financial success is to you.

EXERCISE TWO: EMOTIONAL CHECK-IN AND YOUR MONEY SCRIPT

This exercise is help you develop greater self-awareness about your feelings around money and any money scripts that are influencing you.

1. Take five minutes to describe in your journal your emotional responses to the following prompts:
   - When I think about checking my bank account, I feel . . .
   - Spending money makes me feel . . .
   - Saving money makes me feel . . .
   - Growing up, I was taught that money was . . .
2. Reflect on your early experiences around money. Write down the messages you received (directly or indirectly) growing up. For each one, answer the following questions:
   - Where did this belief come from?
   - Is it true for you now?
   - How is it helping or hurting you?
   - How has it shaped your behavior?
   - What is one thing you'd like to do differently?

EXERCISE THREE: MONEY AND CONTROL

This exercise is meant to evaluate where you feel out of control with your money and where you feel in control. Think about your closest relationships (partner, parents, boss), and answer the following questions and how you feel about each one.

- Who controls the financial decisions?

- Do you feel equal or dependent?
- What one step can you can take to reclaim control or feel more empowered, whether it's having a conversation, asking questions, or opening your own account?

EXERCISE FOUR: FINANCIAL SELF-CHECK

This exercise is intended to make sure you are proactive and know what is happening with your money.

Do a simple evaluation of your current financial habits:
- Do I know my monthly income? _____
- Do I track my spending? _____
- Do I have a savings plan? _____
- Do I understand my debt situation? _____
- Do I know my credit score? _____

Pick one area to improve this week. Keep it small and doable (for example, download a free budget app or review one credit card statement).

EXERCISE FIVE: BUILD A FINANCIAL GOAL

This exercise is to help you to feel financially empowered and set a goal to take at least one action towards financial success and confidence.

Using the SMART method—that is, your goal should be *specific, measurable, achievable, relevant,* and *time-bound*—to write out one financial goal.

Example: *Save $3,000 for a solo retreat by December.*

Then list three steps you'll take this week to get started.

GOAL: _____

1. _____
2. _____
3. _____

Chapter 10
Master Time and Energy to Achieve Life Balance

People often ask me how I manage to do all of the things that I do. I think it might be a second superpower that I've developed, because when I say I'm going to do something, I actually do it. The truth is, I have several time management strategies, but without being clear on what is most important to me and constantly relying on my self-discipline, they would not be useful.

I'm one of those people—I believe they call us idealists—that charge ahead full force with different ideas. I'm always coming up with something new that I want to learn or do. Whether it's creating a coaching program, writing a book, working with clients, or planning for a family vacation, I'm always working on something.

Nevertheless, I've learned that in general, I can only do those things between 9 a.m. and 3 p.m.: the exact hours when my three children attend school. I work hard to stay focused and on task during the day so that when school ends, I can be present and enjoy being with my family without feeling guilty or frustrated.

In 2015, I wrote a book called *Find Your Balance Point*. Its premise is that in order to be the most productive, you have to invest your time and energy in a way that reflects what is most important to you at the time. Having children made me realize that above all I wanted to be a good mother, which meant, to me, having a healthy connection with each of my children (and my husband, of course). I decided that the only way I could achieve that was by giving them each undivided attention on a regular basis. This led me to start weekly dates with each of them. If for whatever reason I couldn't have a date with one of them, I would feel guilty and distracted at work. This is how I determined that I needed to set boundaries on my personal and professional time. I needed to be clear about when I was in "work" mode versus when I was in "mom" mode. The school day became a natural guide for me and created a structure for my time management and productivity. For me, it was my work versus my values around being a mom, but I know that each woman needs to determine what interferes with her ability to focus.

I'm also a huge believer in planning ahead and making lists. I plan my week out every Sunday, my day out every morning, and constantly work backwards to make sure I complete the most pressing task first. Planning makes all the difference in how much you achieve with your time. You know how much I love talking about being proactive—well, your plan lets you be proactive. Your backup plan lets you adapt when plans change or circumstances alter your trajectory (and believe me, I've set many goals with deadlines that had to be adjusted). You learn that you don't quit, you develop self-discipline, and you just find ways to keep the momentum. Time management is life management.

Time Is a Limited Resource

If there is one thing I've learned, it's that time and energy are two of the most valuable resources we have. You can't make more hours: we all have the same twenty-four hours each day. Once the hours are spent, you don't get them back. It's how we use those hours that makes all the difference.

The idea that time is your most precious resource forces you to stop and think about how you are spending it. When you spend your time doing things that matter and are meaningful to you, you feel good and fulfilled. If you spend your time distracted, not pursuing goals, and reacting to others' wants, needs, and demands, you end up feeling sad and frustrated.

The secret is to determine what you want in every area of your life and make sure that on a daily basis you spend your time in a way that reflects what is most important to you. We talked about setting goals and having targets to work towards. This chapter is about how you can keep the momentum in working towards those goals while juggling your many roles and responsibilities.

You will learn how to overcome procrastination, be efficient with your time and schedule, and achieve balance between the many facets of your life. Managing time and energy effectively will allow you to pursue success without sacrificing balance. We will also explore the importance of embracing progress over perfection and celebrating your wins to support momentum and motivation.

Your Balance Point

What makes you feel grounded and balanced is different from what makes me feel grounded and balanced. It's not that one way is better than the other; it's that we are each unique women with different values, experience, preferences, and relationships. We are not juggling the same tasks and therefore will not have the same ideal work-life balance.

It's important to embrace this fact because it is too easy to start comparing yourself to someone else and think they do more, have more, or somehow do things better then you. It's not true, and no matter what, you always have to consider the whole package. If someone is succeeding in one area, they may not be investing as much time and energy in another. You can't be everywhere all at once, so every day you are making a series of choices with how you use your time, and those choices are based on what you need to feel grounded and balanced.

> *It is too easy to start comparing yourself to someone else and think they do more, have more, or somehow do things better then you.*

Have you ever stopped to think about what makes you feel balanced? How much exercise do you need? How many hours of sleep ensure that you wake up feeling refreshed? If you are working, how much time does your work demand of you during the day? How much time does it take to maintain the important relationships in your life? You need to know this in advance in order to plan your time. The more you know in advance, the easier it will be to be productive.

Plan in Advance

Planning your time in advance gives you clarity about your actions. If you don't act with intention, you start doing things that don't move you towards what you want. You may accomplish many tasks, but if they are not meaningful to you, you will feel that you've wasted your time.

Here is a great example: You decide you want to work on a job from home. As you sit there on your computer, your eyes wander, and you notice the laundry that needs to be folded or the dishes on the counter. Maybe you see something out of place and think about putting it away. But you look back at your computer and remember that you have a plan. If you hadn't decided to complete this specific task, you might instead spend the day dealing with household chores. This scenario will play out over days, weeks, months, and years.

In January, I get a big wall calendar with different colored stickers. I take several hours going through the schedules for my children's schools, looking at family and work travel, and noting any significant events during the year. I mark the important dates with different colored stickers, so when I look at the calendar I can see when I'm traveling, when I have important work events, and when significant family moments come up. I'm very visual, and being able to see everything at a glance helps me stay focused and on top of my responsibilities.

I recommend this practice to all my clients. I find that keeping track of your schedule on a digital device is handy when you are moving around, but it can feel overwhelming and cause anxiety when you don't see what you need to do.

I also use a paper planner; my favorite is one called Planner Pad, although of course you can use whichever one you want. Using a pen to write down what you hope to achieve is like setting mini goals: you remember more and hold yourself accountable in a different way. Every Sunday I sit down with my planner and plan out the week. I've already done an overview of the month, so I refer to my month to determine what my week will look like. As I mentioned earlier, I try to keep all my work tasks between 9 a.m. and 3 p.m. so that I can maintain a morning routine with my kids and be available in the afternoon for quality time and other "mother" type jobs. I know what I need to do in order to stay balanced (my own personal balance point) in my mind, body, and heart so I make sure to schedule exercise, self-care, professional development, and time for relationships.

In short, I've found that writing out your goals for the week and a list of to-dos for each day helps you stay focused, organized, and motivated.

Writing out your goals for the week and a list of to-dos for each day helps you stay focused, organized, and motivated.

Complete the Task

Research says that when you complete a task, you release dopamine, which activates the reward center in your brain. Completing a task gives you a boost of confidence and happiness, which motivates you to complete another task. If you have a clear list of to-dos, you will work through them efficiently. The best course of action is to put the hardest or least desired task at the top of your list: once you complete that task, everything else will come easier to you. Think about removing the biggest rock first so the little ones are easy to get through.

The biggest difference between people who are successful and those who aren't is that successful people complete their tasks. You'd be shocked to learn that the majority of people complete a task 90 percent of the way, and then, for whatever reason, they stop and never finish. Just so you know, I'm not immune to this fault. I've pursued several projects that I never finished. I've gotten distracted or lacked information or skills and never got back to them. Those tasks are a weight you drag with you, as opposed to the feeling of elation and pride that comes with successfully completing a major goal. I strive to start and finish a task from beginning to end each time. On days that I do, I accomplish more and feel greater fulfillment.

Successful people complete their tasks.

Do It Now

Don't let yourself procrastinate. If you don't want to do something—especially something that may be challenging or frustrating—it's easy to come up with a million reasons not to. Part of this is because you may be afraid that you won't succeed, or you may prefer to accomplish easier tasks first. But when you are presented with a task you must do, whether it's one of your goals or something that has serious consequences if not done, just do it.

I've embraced the idea of doing it now. When some task presents itself, don't wait or procrastinate; just do it in that moment and get it done. When we defer tasks to another, more convenient time, we often forget to do them, and they pile up on the mountain of "I'll get to it." What is worse is that when you don't do the task immediately, you often forget, and then you have to deal with unwanted consequences. Believe me, you achieve more in less time if you do it now and do it to completion.

Start with the End in Mind

One of the most helpful ways to stay proactive with your time and not lose momentum is to start with the end in mind. When you identify what it takes to complete the project, you can better determine the steps needed to get there and can give each step a deadline. You can also look at several projects at once and coordinate the timing of tasks for each project.

For example, I'm writing this book, and the manuscript is due to the publisher at the end of June. My oldest daughter is graduating from high school at the beginning of June, and my family is taking a trip in July. Knowing I have those three projects, I can chart out what I need to do and in what order to coordinate each event: when I invite family, plan dinner, and order cap and gown for the graduation; when I plan the family trip and make sure we have tickets, valid passports, and accommodations; and how to maintain the targets of my writing schedule so that my manuscript is ready by the deadline. It's like reaching for the balls one at time rather than catching them as they fly at your face.

Navigating Obstacles

One of the biggest obstacles in keeping momentum and managing time is losing confidence in our ability to get the task done. Questioning yourself or your choices throws you off and makes it hard to stay disciplined. You have to commit to positive self-talk. Remind yourself that you are making choices with your time and that those choices represent something meaningful to you. These are things you want to have, be, or do for yourself or your family. You have to believe that what you are working towards is possible. The more you see it as a reality in your imagination, the more motivated and enthusiastic you will feel. Remember, when you have positive expectations about the outcome, you feel positive emotions, which lead to confident, enthusiastic action.

When you find yourself questioning whether you can do the job or not, remind yourself of all the amazing things you've already achieved and envision the success in your mind.

The Growth Mindset

Sometimes people quit because they try something and it doesn't work, so they decide it never will. Accomplished people know that you fail your way to success: things not working out is inevitable. You try something and see how it works; then you make an adjustment and do it better. Adopting a growth mindset means accepting that setbacks are unavoidable and seeing them as learning opportunities. Anything you need to know you can learn, and no one is an expert in the beginning. Everything is hard at the start. With time and experience you get better and understand more, so things become easier. Allow yourself the time to learn what you need to learn to do what you want to do.

Anything you need to know you can learn.

Self-Discipline

When things are hard to do, it's easier to stop or wait for a better time. If you are a busy person, there may never be a better time for you. Self-discipline comes from within, from a desire to want something, and keeps you on track

Some people fuel their self-discipline with accountability to themselves, and others enforce their self-discipline by being accountable to others. To be more productive, a good strategy is to identify what kind of accountability works best for you. You may want to recruit an accountability partner or tell someone your plan so you feel accountable to another person, not just yourself.

Knowing why you are doing something is a powerful way to reinforce your self-discipline. Often when people lose their momentum or become distracted, it's because they've lost touch with why they are doing what they are doing. You need to know why your actions matter and how they fit into the big picture of what you want. You may have decided to work towards something, only to realize that you actually want something different, and that's why you've lost motivation.

Periodically reevaluating your goals, even yearly or monthly goals, is important, because things change, you change, and life happens. Suddenly what seemed important at one point may seem less so with new information. That is part of the growth mindset: accepting that you need to course-correct with new information and experience. I love the concept of course-correcting. The simple act of setting a goal or identifying a target can provide you with focus and direction. How you get there might change, but by giving yourself permission to adjust and adapt, you will become more resilient and likely to arrive at your destination.

The Carrot or the Stick

Whether you have a great deal of self-discipline or you need to be accountable to someone else in order to stay disciplined, you need to know what motivates you. Some people are motivated by praise and reward—the carrot—while others need punishment and consequences—the stick—to keep them moving. Determining what kind of person you are will help you manage your time, overcome obstacles and stay focused despite challenges and distractions.

For women who need to generate their own motivation to accomplish a task, it can be helpful to reflect on the consequences of not doing it in order to fuel the fire of motivation. For others, it might be more beneficial to focus on the reward and use positive reinforcement. Ultimately, you are either running towards something (reward) or away from something (consequence). Which have you found to be more motivating for you: the fear of consequences or the joy of reward?

Celebrate the Wins along the Way

Your goal is to keep the momentum, which can be harder when the task is big or tough to accomplish. A great strategy for keeping the momentum is to break a large task into smaller parts that appear easier or more doable. That way, you don't have to motivate yourself to complete the whole task, only part of it, and when you do, to acknowledge and celebrate the wins along the way.

Staying Focused

You can become skilled at organizing and managing your time and you can build confidence to help you navigate setbacks, but you still need to stay focused. We live in a time when many things cause us to lose focus, and we are constantly having to reset and "lock in," as my children say. Whether it's anticipating and avoiding distractions, managing stress and overstimulation, or avoiding guilt, fighting to stay focused on the task is a challenge all its own. But it is crucial for achieving your goals and feeling fulfilled.

Anticipate and Avoid Distractions

To be most productive, you need to set aside time and space to get things done. It's very challenging to start a task, have to stop to take care of something else, and then come back and restart the task.

Ideally, you start and finish a task all in one fell swoop. It's the most efficient and productive use of your time. To do this, you must anticipate and avoid distractions. If you know you need to do something else such as: make a call, send an email, coordinate child care, before you can give yourself the time and space for the task, do it and get it done so you are not thinking about it and it doesn't become a distraction.

Ideally, you start and finish a task all in one fell swoop.

Earlier I mentioned the idea of starting with the end in mind; you can do this with your day as well. Look ahead, determine all that needs to be done that day, and organize your time and actions so that you complete inevitable tasks that might distract you in advance so you can focus on the most important item.

Here is an example: whenever I need to create a presentation, I know I need a three-hour block of time to allow myself the space to be creative and organize my ideas. Since I know the amount of time I need, I can organize my day with a three-hour window without distractions. I get certain tasks done first, I delegate certain tasks to someone else, and then I make sure to show up for that window of time and stay focused.

Avoid social media and set a schedule for checking your emails or listening to voicemail. Remember, you are planning your days and making to-do lists because you want to be proactive with your time. If you check your email, you will get distracted and start responding to other people or other tasks; then you will be off-track and lose focus. If you commit to checking email and social media only at certain times, you stay in control of your time. You can even manage other people's expectations by telling them in advance when you check your email, so they are aware of your boundaries.

Working from home is a huge distraction, so when you do, make sure you have a designated area that you use specifically for working. When you get into the habit of consistently working in the same space, you can shift into work mode more easily and stay more focused. Keep your work area clean and reduce clutter. You can put up a partition or some other barrier that makes the space feel contained. Ideally, you don't want to be able to see the laundry, the dishes, or the hundred other things that need to be done.

Want to, Have to, and Delegating

Get into the habit of evaluating your to-do list and determining which things you have to do versus the things you want to do. Sometimes we take on tasks and feel compelled to complete them, but having a long list of tasks can cause stress and overwhelm. When you feel overwhelmed, take a look at your list and separate out the tasks that are necessary—the ones that would have consequences if they were not completed—versus those that are optional. Focus on getting the "have to" tasks done first, and then shift to the "want to" tasks. Also evaluate your list for anything that you can delegate to someone else. You don't always have to do everything on your own.

The Guilt Goblin

When you are busy, you constantly have to make choices about where you put your effort and energy. As a result, you are also constantly plagued with the little voice in your head (I like to call it the "guilt goblin") that asks if you have made the right choice and tries to make you question and feel bad about your choices. Should you have pushed the meeting back so you could have driven the kids to school? Should you have volunteered to take on more of the project so you could impress your colleagues? Should you have agreed to have dinner with your friends even though it means not seeing your partner? Most of the time, these questions come up because we are evaluating the past, taking inventory of our regrets, and lacking confidence in our choices.

Since you have proactively made choices based on what is important to you, when you evaluate your choices, you also have reasons for why you made them in the first place. You know why you are doing what you are doing, and this "why" reflects what is meaningful to you. Checking in with the "why" affirms that you made the right choice at the time and helps you feel more confident about your actions. When you plan your time and create your to-do list, you can also add a simple "why" next to the task or connect your tasks to the larger goals you are hoping to achieve. If you feel guilty and need reassurance, you can go back, see why you made those choices, and cut yourself some slack.

Personally, I try to have a consistent morning and evening routine that allows me to check in with my kids and husband. In the morning, I go and wake up each of my kids, and my girls let me cuddle with them. Then I sit on the couch with my husband in our living room and drink coffee. Often my kids will get ready for school and come down and sit with us so we can talk about the day and check in. Then it's off to school and our busy days.

In the evening, we try to have dinner as a family at the table, as often as after-school tennis, volleyball, and theater will allow. At bedtime, I go room to room and spend a couple of minutes checking in with each kid and saying goodnight to them. Finally, I end the evening watching an action-adventure TV show with my husband.

This ritual allows me to start my day feeling grounded and connected to my family and end my day reconnecting with them after each of us has gone about with our own individual plans. I often recommend a check-in, big or small, to busy women trying to juggle all that they do. It's very hard to feel free to pursue your ambition when you feel guilty about not spending time with the people in your life or feeling disconnected from them. When you implement the daily check-in, you will notice right away how much less guilt you feel and how much more focus you have when you are working on your tasks.

Overstimulation, Stress, and Focus

In chapter 8, we talked about paying attention to what causes you stress and different ways to manage it. Managing your stress and noticing when you are feeling overwhelmed or overstimulated is also very important for staying focused and productive. When you feel overstimulated, it's hard to stay focused on a task, because your stamina is drained and your battery is dying.

Stress is inevitable, so you can anticipate it and plan a counterattack by scheduling activities or windows of time that will allow you to decompress and take necessary breaks. Even taking a fifteen-minute walk outside will increase your ability to focus and be productive. I have a neighbor who works from home. Whenever she gets stuck in her work or feels overwhelmed, she takes a walk around the block. It gives her a break and helps her reset her focus. What are some minibreaks you can take during the day that will help you reset your focus?

What are some minibreaks you can take during the day that will help you reset your focus?

Summary

I'm sure you've heard the quote, "It's not about the destination, it's about the journey." Too often we get invested in the outcome, forgetting that every step along the way leads us to the destination and is therefore meaningful. Every time we fail as well as every time we succeed, we are moving towards a goal, and each moment makes up a lifetime. Don't worry about it being perfect: if we only ever took action when we knew it would be perfect and succeed, we'd probably spend a lot of time stuck in the same place and never achieve what we hope to achieve.

It's about progress over perfection. Just commit to taking action, one baby step at a time. When things aren't working or happening fast enough, evaluate and determine if you have to change course or move a little bit slower. As long as you have reflected on all that you want to have, be, or do and are working towards meaningful goals, you will feel fulfilled by your actions and proud of your accomplishments.

Again, it's about choosing how you spend your time in a way that reflects what is most important to you. Stay focused, manage distractions, and keep the momentum by remembering your "why" and celebrating the wins along the way. Whether you're fueled by rewards or consequences, self-discipline and planning in advance are key to staying on track. Don't worry about being perfect; just commit to progress. Take action, one baby step at a time, and remember that your time and energy are limited resources. Use them in ways that make you feel fulfilled, grounded, and aligned with what matters most.

Step Ten
Manage Your Time, Stay Focused, and Live a Balanced Life

Action Plan and Exercises

It's reflection time so get your stuff and get ready to integrate these ideas into your life. You need your journal, guide, pen, and time set aside.

EXERCISE ONE: YOUR WEEKLY PLANNING RITUAL

This exercise is to help you become more proactive with your time and more productive on a daily basis. The most important thing is to feel good about how you spend your time. Identifying why your tasks have meaning will reinforce your motivation and conviction, so you will avoid guilt and feel fulfilled on a daily basis.

Each Sunday, take fifteen to thirty minutes to:
- Review your monthly calendar.
- Write down your top three goals for the week and why they matter to you.
- Schedule your tasks in your ideal work window (for example, 9 a.m. to 3 p.m.). Include time for relationships, exercise, and self-care.

Goal: To build a consistent planning routine that aligns your tasks with your values and keeps you on track.

EXERCISE TWO: COMPLETE THE HARDEST TASK FIRST

This exercise is to help you prioritize your tasks and boost your focus and motivation by encouraging you to complete the hardest, least appealing task first. Each time you complete a task, you activate the reward center in your brain, which propels you to complete another task. Ultimately you boost your productivity.

List your to-dos for the day. Now circle the one you're *least excited* about and *most resistant* to do even though completing this task will have the biggest impact on your day or week. Do that task first. Reflect and journal on what it was like to push yourself to complete the hardest task.

Goal: To trigger momentum, boost confidence, and get into a flow state by activating the brain's reward system early in your day.

EXERCISE THREE: CARROT OR STICK REFLECTION

The purpose of this exercise is help you connect with what motivates you to develop self-discipline and stay on task. Once you know how to motivate yourself, you will be empowered to keep the momentum when there are distractions or you feel overwhelmed.

Answer these questions honestly:
- Am I more motivated by rewards (the carrot) or consequences (the stick)?
- What has worked for me in the past: external accountability or my internal drive?

- Based on that, what is one strategy I can implement this week to stay motivated?

Goal: to understand your core motivation style and use it to fuel your follow-through with any task.

EXERCISE FOUR: CELEBRATE THE WINS

When we set a big goal for ourselves, it can be hard to start the momentum, because the finish line is so far in the distance. But if you break a big goal down into smaller, easier steps, it becomes less intimidating and easier to start.

Choose a goal you're working on (personal or professional).

Break it into three to five smaller milestones.

Now decide on a small reward you'll give yourself after each milestone. For example:

Milestone: Write five pages and reward yourself with a one-hour walk with music.

Milestone: Complete a client project and reward yourself with coffee with a friend.

Milestone: Lose five pounds and reward yourself with a gift card to your favorite store.

Goal: To create positive momentum by rewarding progress and making the journey enjoyable.

EXERCISE FIVE: KEEP THE GUILT GOBLIN AWAY

This exercise is meant to help you gauge when you are out of balance with how you are distributing your time. This shows up as you start feeling guilty when you are investing in yourself.

We keep the guilt goblin away by evaluating the goals we set and by identifying why we do them and how each goal reflects something meaningful to us. If your actions are aligned with your values, you will feel more confident and less guilty about your choices.

List five goals or tasks you have for next week.

1.
2.
3.
4.
5.

Next to each goal, write down why achieving it will improve your life.

At the end of the week, reflect on how you felt when you were working on your goals and if you benefited from going back and reminding yourself of the "why" behind what you were doing.

Goal: To make sure you are being proactive with your time and doing tasks that are meaningful to you.

EXERCISE SIX: CREATE A CHECK-IN RITUAL

The purpose of this exercise is to establish a small check-in routine with the people in your life. When you feel connected to them, it is easier to focus on your goals. When you don't, you become distracted and feel guilty about how you are spending your time.

Example: I have a wake-up routine with my kids and coffee in the morning with my husband (for all of ten minutes). At night I have a bedtime routine with my kids and a conversation about the next day with my husband. This is how I check in every day and stay connected.

Think of brief rituals you can establish at the beginning and the end of the day that enable to you check in with your people.

Goal: To establish a routine that makes you feel grounded and connected throughout the day.

Chapter 11
Never Stop Investing In Yourself: The Power of Being a Lifelong Learner

GROWING UP WITH A motivational speaker for a father was like living with a cheerleader. Whenever I questioned my ability to do something or realized I didn't know information I needed to know, he was always there to tell me that he believed in me and he knew that whatever it was, I could figure it out.

I will be honest: I often looked at him with his passionate, steadfast confidence and wondered what it was he saw that I didn't. Still, I trusted him and took the leap of faith, even when I wasn't clear about how I would figure out the problem. This encouragement was helpful in school, because I expected learning to be challenging, but I never doubted my ability to eventually conquer the idea or subject and learn what I needed to. I also developed a work ethic and did not expect things to be easy: I knew that if something was important, you had to work for it.

Unfortunately, I was not a good test taker, so I really did learn how to work for it. In order to get good grades, I had to put out a lot of effort participating in class, writing papers, and pretty much anything else that wasn't a test. My job was to keep learning and overcoming challenges to get to the next level. I embraced learning as an essential component in accomplishing my goals and living a meaningful life.

A Major Identity Shift

Later in life, being a lifelong learner took on a whole new meaning when I had to navigate a major identify shift after becoming a mother. They say that the first year after having a child is the hardest on a couple and, boy, did I learn that. I was excited to become a mother, and I was happy to meet my daughter Julia, but I was shocked to discover all the things they don't tell you about having a baby.

Most significant for me was the complete and utter lack of desire and disconnection from my sexuality. I loved my husband but struggled to find any desire for sex or intimacy. I felt bad and guilty that I couldn't show up for him. I had no idea how important it was to show up as a wife. Up to this point, I did not understand that intimacy in a relationship is more than mere physical pleasure: it is an unspoken validation of connection and commitment. At first, I didn't think it mattered if we were not intimate, but after a long painful conversation, I realized that our lack of intimacy would hurt our relationship. I was reluctant to share this with anyone, but fortunately it came up all on its own.

At the time, I was in a new moms' group. When the subject of sex came up, almost every woman in the room expressed the same lack of desire as well as their shame or guilt about it. I couldn't believe how many women were struggling with the same problem. I knew that this issue extended far beyond our mothers' group. How many other women were suffering in silence, not knowing how to experience desire again? How many partners felt rejected or isolated from their wives after starting their families? In my mind, something had to be done.

I decided to learn about sexual desire—what it was and how you could cultivate it at different stages of life. I did research and learned a lot of theoretical information on the subject, but it wasn't until I decided to take a class at a local erotic boutique that the importance of learning took on a whole new meaning for me.

At the class, I learned about pleasure, and I learned some new and different techniques to provide pleasure. It completely transformed how I felt about intimacy, sexual desire, and my own identity as a sexual being. In learning something new to try, I realized that I had unlocked my enthusiasm, which made me excited and motivated to experience intimacy. The novelty of a new technique not only boosted my confidence but reignited a passion for something that had felt boring and monotonous.

I began teaching women how to reconnect with themselves and bring passion back into their relationships. The core of my workshop was empowering these women with new knowledge and practical skills that gave them increased understanding of themselves, their sexual desire, and their partnerships. Since creating the workshop, I have delivered it to thousands of women, many of whom tell me that gaining accurate information and practical skills has transformed how they experience themselves and their relationships (not to mention saved many marriages). In my quest to bring back desire to myself and my relationship, I learned the power of competency. Knowing you have the ability, knowledge, and skill to do something successfully not only gives you the confidence and motivation to do it but makes you believe in yourself and generates enthusiasm.

I first learned this idea as it relates to relationships and intimacy, but I've since realized that this is the secret to staying engaged and feeling inspired in your life. To be fully engaged in what you do, you have to believe you are capable of contributing value and getting results. You have to commit to being a lifelong learner so that you are constantly gaining new information and generating newfound enthusiasm for what you do. Enthusiasm makes all the difference.

> *Commit to being a lifelong learner so that you are constantly gaining new information and generating newfound enthusiasm.*

Being a Lifelong Learner

The eleventh step to living life on your own terms is to never stop learning and being curious. This enables you to continually find ways to generate enthusiasm in all that you do. In addition, the more you know, the more choices you have. Throughout history, those who have had the knowledge have had the power—not just power over others, but the power to pursue goals and improve their own lives. I want you to feel truly empowered. To do that, you must pursue subjects and skills that will improve every aspect of your life at every stage.

As children, we go to school to learn basic subjects. Many of us then earn degrees to help us get jobs so we are able to take care of ourselves. For many people, their learning journey stops there. They become passive and simply maintain the status quo

That is a choice, but if you want to feel fulfilled, inspired, and engaged, you have to invest in yourself through constant growth and development, physically, emotionally, and mentally.

Lifelong learning is a way of being. It's about adopting a growth mindset and believing that you can learn anything you want through effort, practice, and persistence. People with a growth mindset integrate learning into daily life, whether it's self-reflection and learning about your own personal psychology or professional development through courses, mentorship, and podcasts.

You can develop your abilities, talents, and intelligence in many different ways. In fact, one of the gifts of the Covid pandemic was that we had to adapt and make more information available online. Many workshops, conferences, and trainings had to be translated into a digital format. This means that continuing your education in any field is now more accessible than it ever was. The educational resources available now empower you to learn anything you want. We have thousands of podcasts focused on every subject imaginable, and authors across the board writing books and following them up with online courses and downloadable workbooks. In some cases, we've even shifted from longer-format videos to microlearning videos, which enable you to take ten minutes a day to learn a new subject. I know you can find ten minutes in your day to commit to learning something new.

Where could you incorporate a space for learning in your schedule? Could you read a book while drinking coffee in the morning? Could you listen to a podcast while driving? Maybe you could sign up for an online course and do one session every evening before bed instead of watching TV.

When you commit to being a lifelong learner, you foster adaptive thinking so you can embrace the inevitable changes through different phases of life as the world continues to change and evolve. Change is scary for most people, because they become comfortable with what they know (remember the comfort zone). The idea of having to navigate the unknown triggers the thought that you don't know *how* or you don't know *what* to do. When you adopt a growth mindset, you learn to embrace change, which scares you less because you are curious and seek to expand your understanding or learn a new skill. Maybe you see it as taking an old way of thinking or doing and adapting it to become more relevant. You know and trust that your skills will improve through effort and practice and that failure is a part of the learning process and an opportunity to grow. Challenges make you stronger, and you welcome feedback as valuable information that empowers you to adapt and try new approaches.

When you adopt a growth mindset, you learn to embrace change.

You can adopt a growth mindset even if you've spent most of your life believing that things are the way they are and they don't change and you are satisfied with what you know or are good at. With a growth mindset, you reframe that self-talk. You replace the idea that you can't to do something with the idea that you can't do it *yet*. You might not know now, but you will be able to once you understand how. Just as we talked about rewarding yourself for achieving milestones on the way to your goals, with a growth mindset you also acknowledge the process of learning. It's not just about what you want to achieve but it's also about the effort and commitment needed along the way.

It's not easy to learn something new or develop a skill: it requires commitment on your end, making time for practicing and applying what you learn. You have to encourage yourself to take on the challenge, and stay with it until you've succeeded. I guarantee that you will feel proud of yourself when you push yourself to learn something, apply the new skill, and see the results of your effort. It really does light a spark of excitement.

As a lifelong learner, you are constantly looking for ways to experience personal or professional growth, because you know that it helps you engage in what you are doing and imbues your actions with more meaning and purpose. You want to live a fulfilling life, you want to be in control, and you want to look back on what you've accomplished and feel proud to pass it on. It starts with becoming a lifelong learner and a student of your own life.

Become a Student of Your Own Life

How can you be a student of your own life? Traditionally a student is a person who is enrolled in an institution like a college, university, or school, and studies a particular subject for a specific reason. Once they have attained their degree or completed the course, their learning journey ends.

I like to think of a student as someone who makes the choice to study, investigate, and explore anything that might be relevant in their lives—throughout their lives. I've created a guide based on the acronym STUDENT to show you what you will gain from this commitment.

So what does it mean to be a **STUDENT**? It means that you:

Spark curiosity that opens your mind and builds connection with others.

Trust your capacity to grow, knowing that your brain is always changing and you are capable of learning and adapting at any age.

Unlock the power of purpose by choosing what you learn and aligning it with what matters most.

Design your learning journey through every life phase, setting goals that reflect your evolving needs.

Embrace emotional intelligence and personal growth by staying curious about yourself and creating more meaningful relationships.

Novelty is the key to igniting excitement, sparking motivation, and bringing joy to the present moment.

Transformation is a part of life. Every challenge, every phase, and every discovery is part of becoming who you are meant to be. Let's explore this in more detail.

Being a STUDENT

Spark curiosity.
Trust your capacity to grow.
Unlock the power of purpose.
Design your learning journey.
Embrace emotional intelligence.
Novelty is the key to igniting excitement.
Transformation is a part of life.

S: Spark Curiosity

Children are naturally curious. They constantly want to understand what things are, how they work, and why they are important.

Their curiosity makes them see everything, not just the familiar things in front of them. It's like sitting in the back seat of your car and paying attention not just to the route, watching the buildings, trees and people as you drive, but to all the details of the car that you've never noticed before. To be a student of your life, you need to be curious, you need to ask questions, you need to seek greater understanding of things around you and what they mean to others.

As we age and settle into our daily lives and patterns, we grow more attached to our perspectives and values. We assume that the meaning we make out of something is the same for everyone; we don't stop to think that they may feel differently or do something differently for their own reasons. But when you are curious, you learn how to act in many different ways, and each question you ask leads you to another question. Pretty soon you find yourself on a treasure hunt for ideas, perspectives, and possibilities.

When you are curious about another person and seek to understand them for who they are, you deepen the relationship and foster greater connection. There is something very powerful about being seen and validated by someone else. Your openness and acceptance through curiosity builds community. It makes your day more joyful, gives you greater confidence, and fuels a passion for discovery. The more curious you are about the world beyond the familiar, the more you seek to understand, the more relevant and adaptable you will be. Ask questions and come up with new ideas. It's how we evolve and make greater meaning.

T: Trust Your Capacity to Grow

Your brain is always changing, which means you can learn and adapt at any age. Research on neuroplasticity shows that the brain can develop and evolve by forming new neural connections in response to experiences and stimuli throughout your life. Your brain thus adapts to new experiences, incorporates new skills, and even reorganizes and recovers from injury. The anti-aging movement encourages people to continue learning as a way to keep the mind healthy and prevent deterioration. If you want to keep your mind sharp, you have to exercise it like a muscle, and you do it by continual learning. Through problem-solving, memorizing, and taking in new information, your brain develops those new connections.

The science is there to prove that you have the ability to learn and grow. You can tackle challenges, learn a new language, or develop any skill you want. Even if a particular subject is harder than another, that doesn't mean it's impossible: it just means you have to work a little harder. In his book *David and Goliath: Underdogs, Misfits, and the Art of Battling Giants*, Malcolm Gladwell talks about how people can learn to overcome all kinds of disability and adversity. In fact, they often learn new ways of doing things that make them even more capable than if they had learned the traditional way. We have the ability to adapt, learn, and grow in many different ways. There is no right or wrong way to learn, only different ways. There are no limitations but the ones you put on yourself.

U: Unlock the Power of Purpose

I remember going to my freshman orientation at university. A professor got up and spoke to all the new students, who were eager to begin this new phase of their learning journey. Some of us were clear about what we wanted to study; some of us arrived open to many possibilities. I was surprised when the professor told us that in his experience, students changed their major three times before they knew which direction they wanted to take. They pursued specific tracks of learning and switched three times over the course of four years. Each class, each discussion, each project the student engaged in moved them one step closer to knowing which track was meant for them and where they wanted to focus their effort. Students needed to take a range of classes to figure out which ones they enjoyed and which ones failed to inspire them. Each time they took a class they enjoyed, it would lead to another class, which would enable them to go even deeper in that field, getting closer and closer to clarity about their professional pursuits.

Being a student of your life is much like attending university—only as an adult, you don't have to take a class; you get to choose which "classes" you take. You can connect with what you are interested in and learn more. When you find meaning in your studies, you achieve deeper comprehension and connection to the material. With that, you become more motivated and aligned with a sense of purpose and fulfillment. Whether it's becoming a better parent, improving your relationship, gaining more specific knowledge in your field, or learning a completely new skill, each step on your learning journey engages you in what you do and gives you a greater sense of purpose.

Think about all you do. In what area of your life do you feel you could expand? What one thing right now do you want to learn more about? What is one skill that, if you improved it, would make the biggest difference in your life?

D: Design Your Learning Journey

Earlier we explored the idea that people who have goals have a greater sense of direction and feel more in control of their lives.

Both adults and children thrive when they feel in control of their learning and skill development. The more empowered you are, the greater satisfaction and investment you will feel in the process. Your choices will change and you will set different goals, because what is relevant to your learning journey will evolve throughout your life. You will want and need to learn more about each life phase you are in so you can know how to navigate it confidently. These life phases reflect both your personal journey and your professional journey.

Let's take one woman's journey as an example. This girl grows up studying a range of subjects while attending elementary school and then graduating from high school: her whole life is one big possibility. She becomes a young woman, falls in love, and gets married. Soon after, she and her husband choose to have kids. At this point, her learning goal might be about pregnancy, childbirth, and raising young children. After the baby arrives, they embrace parenthood and decide to have a second child. The next goal might be learning about relationship skills, sexual desire, and how to have a happy family. Maybe she becomes interested in nutrition and learns how to cook and make healthy meals for her family. Time passes, and she may decide to coach a kids' soccer team, so she needs to learn the game. Or she decides to go back to work, and she needs to update her skills to be relevant and confident on the job.

Years later, the children have graduated and are out of the house. The woman goes through a major identity shift and has to rediscover herself, so she takes classes on personal psychology, works with a therapist, and begins journaling to reflect on her thoughts and feelings. She realizes she wants to travel. She learns all the ins and outs of travel, assuring her husband she can get them the best deals. Her learning includes exploring different countries and cultures so she can appreciate their traditions and understand their cultural norms.

This woman hits forty-five, and her body starts changing in ways she would not have chosen and does not fully understand. Now she needs to learn about aging, changing hormones, and the importance of weight training. She hires a personal trainer to teach her how to eat and exercise in order to keep her muscles strong and protect her bones.

Fast-forward, and now she is sixty-five and has four grandchildren. Her life is completely different now: she is retired, and she gets to choose what keeps her busy. She loves crossword puzzles and is learning Spanish. She knows it's important to keep her brain sharp. She still exercises, but now that she is older, she has had to learn new ways of staying strong. She has learned that staying connected to her community keeps people happy as they age, so she has moved into a community for older people. She and her husband play bridge (a game she had to learn, since she'd never played before) with the neighbors. Her life has felt fulfilling, because every step of the way she embraced what she needed to learn to do what she wanted.

This woman's path is unique to her, but each of us has our own path. Stay aware of opportunities that present themselves at each phase. That way, you can proactively set goals and fortify your sense of purpose, enabling you to take each new step.

Stay aware of opportunities that present themselves at each phase of life.

E: Emotional Intelligence and Personal Growth

You are constantly changing. Every day you have experiences that shape who you are, whether it's the way you do something or the conversations you have. You are evolving on a daily basis. Being a student of life also means exploring your own thoughts and feelings, discovering factors that influence your preferences and those that causes you distress. We all have rich, multifaceted histories with narratives from other people about who we are or should be. We have a lifetime of experiences, some that have been good, some that have been bad. Either way, they shape our subconscious bias and influence us all the time. The key is to gain awareness of the elements that have contributed to who we are, and then evaluate what still remains true now versus what needs to be released.

Personal growth is about staying open to the fact that you don't know everything and you are not always right. You want to be curious, not just about the world around you, but also about yourself. Why do you do certain things? Why do you react to some things and care less about others? Why are you drawn to certain people and find others annoying or frustrating? You have an opportunity to be a student of yourself so that you can continue to grow and have deeper experiences with the people around you.

Emotional intelligence is something you cultivate, and the more you do, the more capable you will become of having deep connections and meaningful relationships. For example, people with high emotional intelligence learn to pause in an exchange that provokes a big emotional reaction. They reflect on the feeling and ask themselves, "Is this familiar? If so, where does it come from?" They are able to self-reflect and track the source of their reaction so they can choose how they respond. This intentional response takes into account both how they are feeling and how the response may affect the other person. Going through this process sets you up to stay connected in your conversations while still honoring your own internal experience.

Another important concept in emotional intelligence is "snowballing," whereby a negative thought or feeling rapidly transforms into a big emotion. You prevent snowballing by noticing your reactions and pausing before you add to the feeling with supporting evidence (in essence building up the snowball). You stop yourself and evaluate only the facts: not what *could* happen, only what *has happened*. You stop the snowball from building and launching at full speed down a slippery slope right into full-blown panic. Pausing to stop snowballing helps to regulate your nervous system so you remain calm and present and allows you to make space for the other person's experience and reality.

Developing your emotional intelligence gives you an appreciation for the unique experience of others. You learn to appreciate and embrace different ways of thinking and feeling instead of feeling threatened by them. It starts with learning about yourself and the exchange of emotions within yourself and within others.

N: Novelty Ignites Excitement

If you do the same thing every day in the same way, it doesn't matter how much you love it: if you know what to expect, it leaves little to anticipate. This is true for your daily routine, your relationship, your job, or whatever else you do on a regular basis. Even your exercise routine will become boring and less effective.

That's where novelty comes in. When you learn something new, your brain releases dopamine, which gives you feelings of pleasure, satisfaction, and motivation. It generates excitement and anticipation for more discovery. It also helps you become more mindful, because you are more focused and present when you are doing something you've never done before.

Think about that: doing something new makes you feel rewarded and forces you to be present. We know through research on happiness that people who live in the now and focus on the present are happier and more satisfied with their lives. When you focus on the past, you tend to feel guilt, sadness, and regret from reflecting on loss and missed opportunity. When you focus on the future, you may feel fear and panic as you anticipate some impending doom (although not everyone goes to that place, many people do worry about the future). Staying in the present lets you enjoy the moment and keeps you calm and happy. You keep yourself in the present by staying in the now, and you can set yourself up to be more focused by incorporating novelty.

Seeking out novelty is like going on treasure hunt to see what you will discover. Here is a perfect and easy example: The next time you drive to a place you go to on a regular basis, taking the same route each time, try getting there by a completely different way. You will be amazed to discover new buildings, new trees, maybe even neighborhoods you didn't know existed. You might also enjoy your drive more, because you are present as you look around and make sure you are heading toward your destination. You can try this on your drive, or you can try this at home by approaching regular activities with a new technique or tactic.

If you feel a lack of engagement at work, try learning a new skill that is relevant to your job. You could also do some research into your industry and try a different approach to what you usually do. You will find a new level of engagement and motivation at work.

I mentioned at the beginning of this chapter how trying something new in my relationship reinvigorated my enthusiasm and engagement. Novelty is powerful and easy to incorporate. You can try something easy or something that seems out of your comfort zone or even makes you nervous. Either way, you will trigger dopamine in your brain and feel excited and motivated in a whole new way. You might also feel happy, present, and satisfied.

T: Transformation through Life Phases

One thing we can count on in life is change. We will change, people around us will change, and the world will change. In order to adapt to those changes, we need to embrace lifelong learning.

As women, we navigate many roles, and our identities are constantly evolving. The only way to stay grounded and confident is to be willing to embrace each phase of life. It's not just about managing it or getting through it, but making the most of every phase as you pass through.

Summary

Knowledge is power. Knowing what to expect and how to embrace it will empower you to feel accomplished with each transformation you go through. It's exciting to track your own evolution and reflect on the challenges you've overcome or the identity shifts you've had to navigate. Your transformations are milestones in your life. When you take an inventory of everything you've learned at each phase, you will feel proud of yourself for overcoming, achieving, and embracing who you are and who you've been.

When you choose to be a student of your own life, you approach change, challenge, and transformation with curiosity and a desire to discover yourself in a whole new way. It doesn't mean that change won't feel scary, because the unknown is scary, but if you believe you are capable of absorbing new knowledge and learning new skills, you will move forward with confidence, trust, and an open mind.

Becoming a student of your own life means choosing to grow through every phase with curiosity, purpose, and intention. Learning is not something you just do in school: it's a way of being that helps you stay engaged, inspired, and empowered. When you trust your capacity to grow, unlock meaning in your experiences, and embrace emotional intelligence, you create opportunity in every challenge. Novelty sparks excitement, and each transformation brings the chance to rediscover who you are and what matters most. The more you learn, the more confident and capable you become. Being a lifelong learner gives you power—not just to accomplish your goals, but to feel fulfilled and live life on your own terms.

Step Eleven
Commit to Being a Lifelong Student of Your Own Life

Action Plan and Exercises

Now it's time to reflect and start your personal learning journey. Go get your journal or your guide and prepare for the following exercises.

EXERCISE ONE: CURIOSITY JOURNAL (S = SPARK CURIOSITY)

This exercise will help reignite your sense of wonder and expand your perspective.

Start paying more active attention throughout your day. Try to notice things you stopped paying attention to and cultivate curiosity. Tap into your inner child and engage with your life in a new way.

Exercise: For one week, write down three questions per day that you're genuinely curious about related to your life, your work, your people, or the world around you.

For example, you could ask yourself:
- What's something I've never fully understood but always wanted to?
- Why do I feel energized by some conversations and drained by others?
- What if I did my routine differently tomorrow or eliminated some part of it altogether?
- What is that? How does that work?

Journal prompt: At the end of the week, review your questions and highlight those that feel most meaningful. Choose one to explore further.

EXERCISE TWO: LIFE PHASE GROWTH TIMELINE
(T = TRUST YOUR CAPACITY TO GROW)

This exercise is intended to give you the opportunity to reflect back and take an inventory of all the growth you've gone through at crucial points throughout your life. This will help you recognize your learning, resilience, and adaptability over time and will hopefully inspire you to embrace new learning in the future.

Exercise: Create a timeline of your life in phases (for example, childhood, early adulthood, midlife, now). For each phase, write:

- One challenge you faced
- One skill or mindset you developed
- How you adapted or changed
- How you felt about the experience at the time
- The transformation that occurred

Journal prompt: What do these past learning moments reveal about your strengths today? Where might those strengths still apply?

EXERCISE THREE: PURPOSE ALIGNMENT
(U = UNLOCK THE POWER OF PURPOSE)

The goal of this exercise is to help you connect to your talents and passions and create a guide for pursuing opportunities that will help you develop your unique gifts and share them with the people around you.

1. List 3 things you are good at.
2. List 3 things you are passionate about

Reflection: Write a paragraph about how you use what you are good at to help support the people or causes you are passionate about. What new skills or knowledge can you develop to enhance your sense of purpose and offer even more to those you care about?

EXERCISE FOUR: LEARNING CHART
(D = DESIGN YOUR LEARNING JOURNEY)

Each goal you have or aim you want to achieve will take effort. By acquiring more knowledge and skills, you will become empowered by more choices and the ability to make a greater impact. This exercise will help connect your learning with your values, the why behind the what, and personal or professional goals.

Exercise: Draw a three-column chart with the headings:
- What I want to learn
- Why it matters to me
- How it will affect my life and work

Or use the chart on the next page. Come up with at least five learning objectives.

Reflection: Choose one learning goal and write a paragraph about how it aligns with your deeper sense of purpose or identity.

What I want to learn	Why it matters to me	How it will affect my life and work

EXERCISE FIVE: EMOTION CHECK-IN PRACTICE
(E = EMOTIONAL INTELLIGENCE)

Emotional intelligence is all about self-awareness and emotional regulation. It's amazing how changing the way you think about something changes the way you feel about it.

This exercise is designed for you to track your experiences and notice when you have a big feeling. The goal is to become more aware of your feelings and the circumstances that inspired them. You can reflect and interpret the experience in multiple ways to see if you can regulate your feelings and ultimately your reactions.

Exercise: Each day for one week, pause and reflect when you experience a big emotion. Write answers to the following questions:

- What am I feeling right now?
- What triggered this feeling?
- How is this emotion influencing my thoughts or actions?
- Is there another way to interpret the circumstances?
- If I do this, does it change how I feel about the circumstances and the emotions I have?

Reflection: Look for emotional patterns over the week. Do certain emotions block or fuel your learning? What circumstances cause the biggest emotions (positive or negative)?

EXERCISE SIX: "NEWNESS DARE" (N = NOVELTY)

Trying something new or doing something differently brings new energy into your life and forces you to be present and engaged in the task. Our brains love novelty. You will find newfound enthusiasm when you are you open to growth through new experiences and transforming your habits and actions. If you want to feel truly alive on a daily basis, follow the advice of Eleanor Roosevelt: "Do one thing every day that scares you."

Exercise: Commit to trying one new thing every day this week—big or small.

Examples: Attend a new workshop; start a new book; learn a new skill; have a different kind of conversation; take a new route home; eat a new food; sleep in a different room; call an old friend; try a new kind of exercise listen to a different kind of music. The sky's the limit.

Afterward, answer these questions:
- How did it feel?
- What did I learn (about myself or the world)?
- What surprised me?

Reflection: what transformations might come if you made a habit of doing "new" or "scary" things?

EXERCISE SEVEN: REVIEW A TRANSFORMATION (T: TRANSFORMATION)

Journal prompt: Write about a transformation you have experienced in your life. How were you before, what was the challenge or crisis you went through, and who are you now because of the experience?

12

Design Your Legacy and Live a Meaningful Life

WHAT LEGACY DO YOU want to leave? I was recently asked that question. At first I laughed at the idea that I, little me, would leave a legacy. I thought about my father: he is the kind of person that leaves a legacy. What he has done with his career and his mission though his speaking, writing, and teaching has made a big impact on the world. He has spoken in eighty-six countries and written almost 100 books. Some colleges even use his material as the basis of courses. I can't even imagine coming close to that kind of impact.

Before I was asked this question, I believe I was just satisfied with the idea that my kids seem happy and healthy and that if I raised good people, that would be my legacy. I have now come to see that the legacy of motherhood, while incredibly important, is just one piece of my puzzle.

As I reflected on this question, I realized that I was comparing my contributions to those of famous people who had done "big" things (like my dad) and that I was devaluing the work that I have done and continue to do. I was not acknowledging the importance of the energy I invest in the people and relationships that I hold dear.

I also started to think about the incredible women I know and the amazing things they have done. Not amazing, perhaps, on an Oprah Winfrey scale, but many women I know have cultivated their courage and talents to serve others and make a difference, whether it's within their families, with their communities, or with their work. I realized that the legacy that I leave is uniquely mine, just as the legacy someone else leaves is uniquely theirs. Once I connected to that idea, I started to really appreciate how I've shown up in my life and how I actually have had an impact on the people around me. I am leaving a legacy, whether I've defined it or not. Every day, every action I take becomes a part of this legacy.

A Definite Chief Aim

I thought about the idea of having a "Definite Chief Aim," a concept first introduced in a book that deeply inspired my father: *Think and Grow Rich*, by Napoleon Hill. It explains that the drive which propels you forward, combined with a definitive plan, ultimately becomes your legacy.

My father, for example, originally defined his major purpose as the discovery of why some people were more successful than others. His quest led him to learn all about success and teach people all over the world key concepts in professional achievement. Once he discovered that there was a formula, he felt compelled to teach it to everyone seeking financial freedom and professional success. He was propelled forward by his major defining purpose, and as a result he has left his impact and legacy.

The drive which propels you forward, combined with a definitive plan, ultimately becomes your legacy.

Personally, I've always felt drawn to teach others what I've learned as if they absolutely *must* know. As I've mentioned, this did not serve me to the same degree when I was a preschooler eager to teach my peers where babies came from, but it sure works for me now.

I love teaching people how to release their potential so they can feel successful and empowered and demonstrate the power of showing up as their flawed, vulnerable, authentic selves. I did this when I first decided to speak up about my lack of desire in my relationship. I was terrified, but I came to see that sharing my story gave others permission to share theirs. This in turn helped me realize that it wasn't about me anymore: it was about all women. This all started as a leap of faith and took a bit of bravery on my part, but I'm so glad I took the chance.

The contribution I hope to make is to help as many people as possible, especially women, to reconnect and confidently express themselves with complete authenticity. I want them to be able to embrace all parts of themselves, including their sexual energy—not just for pleasure, but as a way to fully step into themselves and make an impact in the world. I'd like to show others that it's OK to be authentic and that vulnerability actually makes you more likable and easier to connect with. We achieve more together than we do alone, and by lifting others, we all rise.

Your Unique Legacy

In many ways, the little things you do may end up having the greatest impact on your legacy. The way you express yourself, the words you use, and the actions you take will make a difference for someone else, whether you know it or not. It could be as simple as the smile you give the clerk at the gas station or the long hug goodbye before you head off for the day. You might pay a compliment or offer an encouraging insight that completely changes the trajectory of someone else's path. Putting away your phone and choosing to be fully present for your family could change how they value themselves, because you show them that they matter.

Remember, there is no one else like you. You are the only person in the whole world that has your unique perspective, collection of experiences, and voice. You are here now to put your own unique stamp on this planet and the people in your life—the ones you know personally and the ones with whom you cross paths out of circumstance. You have an impact on others in one way or another every single day. When you think about your legacy, ask yourself:

What kind of impact do I want to have?

What does legacy mean to me?

There is no one else like you.

Leadership Is a Part of Your Legacy

Don't underestimate what you know and how important your sharing could be for someone else. That's leadership, and we are all leaders. We lead by example, and we lead by intention. Whether in your home, your business, or your community, your actions have the power to lead others. Leadership is not about your position, it's about how you treat people, the daily decisions you make, and your influence on the actions of others. Your leadership is a part of your legacy, and you get to decide what kind of leader you will be and where you want to lead. Whom can you have the greatest impact on?

You lead with intention when you have the confidence to speak up, act first, or convince others to do something they might not have done without your influence. Speaking up or taking the initiative is scary; there are a million reasons why you might convince yourself to keep quiet or just let things be the way they are. But if you can empower someone else to improve the quality of their life, wouldn't that be worth the risk? And wouldn't it be meaningful for you to know that you had a positive impact on someone else?

Leadership is also about encouraging others to act. Some leaders lead with a capital L: they are bold and take charge, leading the way to achieve the goal. Other leaders lead with a lower-case L: they lead by gently guiding others through example in the direction of success. You don't have to be loud and bold to lead; you can be soft and quiet and still be a powerful leader. You get to be uniquely *you* and do it your way.

How are you a leader at home, at work, with your friends, and in your community?

What actions do you think people take as a result of watching you and how you live your life?

Think about what you know. If by sharing it you could make a difference for someone else, does that excite you or scare you?

How does this all fit into the legacy you want to leave?

Your Legacy of Motherhood

I believe one of the most lasting and powerful forms of contribution is caring for someone else, which brings me back to my legacy as a parent. Too many women underestimate the importance of being a dedicated mother; as a result, they feel they haven't done enough with their lives, or they regret that they didn't make other choices. If you relate to this, please don't compare yourself to other women. Realize that you have chosen to create a family legacy, and that is an accomplishment. Your presence with your children is one the most meaningful things you can do. If all you do is raise them with love and care, that in itself is a legacy to be proud of.

I've gone through phases in my life when my whole focus was raising my children and I was a full-time mom, and I've shifted into phases where I've had to juggle my work with my role as mom.

When I had three children under five, I was not contributing outside of my home: my main focus was showing up as a mother. If that meant dressing up like a princess, coloring, or playing with cars, that's what I did. In retrospect, at that point in my life, I believe I was contributing something meaningful, but I think it's easy to devalue those contributions without seeing how important they are as a part of your legacy. I know I questioned the value of how I was contributing, and it often felt unseen, because I wasn't being paid, but now I can reassure myself that it did matter, and I'm proud of taking that time to play. However, I needed to go back and evaluate the way I contributed at different phases of my life in order to give myself acknowledgment for how I've lived my life. The same is true for you.

How do you feel you are contributing now? How do you feel you've contributed in the past?

What does contributing mean to you?

What legacy are you hoping to leave when it comes to motherhood or caring for others?

How would you want your children to describe you as a mother?

What lessons or feelings from you would you hope they would carry forward into their lives and with their families?

It's not about proving your worth or earning something. It's about feeling you've had a purpose, and you get to determine when and how you fulfill that purpose and how it carries on. The footprint you leave as a parent not only exists in your lifetime but will continue to have an impact on many lifetimes in the future. Think about all the time and energy you put into raising your children, the sacrifices you make to show up, and your dedication to teaching them how to become good people with passion and the ability to make a difference. Your care and investment in those children are not just a part of your legacy, but also a part of theirs. What you contribute as a parent will directly affect how they show up in the world and the legacy they will leave. The time and the moments you spend together will shape how they learn to see love, connection, and family. Your actions will carry into how they love, how they connect, and the families they raise.

I try to live every day as if tomorrow is not guaranteed, and I aim to make every day meaningful. Sometimes that means appreciating traffic as an opportunity to talk longer with my kids on the way home from school or canceling a workout to show up for a client who needs me. Maybe it's getting up early to work on a project so that I have more time to be present with my family during the day. I've identified many different ways in which I show up at home and at work, and I remind myself that they all matter.

If you have decided not have children, but you've cared for others, or you've divided your focus between work and family, your legacy looks different—not better or worse, not right or wrong, only different. Your approach teaches those around you a different set of values and another way of learning to love, connect, and live a life with meaning.

Start with the End in Mind

Imagine yourself at the end of your life (this may sound a little bit morbid, but trust me: it's a powerful exercise). What do you want people to say about you? Not just the accomplishments you've achieved, but the way you made people feel, the values you represented, and how you showed up both personally and professionally.

Imagine yourself at the end of your life. What do you want people to say about you?

If it's hard to think about this for yourself, try reflecting on the life of someone close to you. If you had to write their eulogy and describe the way they lived their life and the gifts they left behind, what would you say? Now imagine if you had to read that eulogy to that close friend. Would they be pleased with how you perceived their life, or would they have wanted to leave a different legacy?

If you are brave, you could even ask someone else right now to write a eulogy for you to give you perspective on the legacy you are currently leaving. You can also try writing your own. Think of it as a legacy guide, helping you align your life now with the one you want to have lived.

Your Legacy Is Your Personal Brand

In a way, designing your legacy is like establishing your own personal brand. You have to envision the brand fully established and realized, and then you can determine all the pieces you need to build it into what you want it to be. (Don't worry about what stage of life you are in: you can always rebrand starting now). How do you do that?

Hopefully you've written your eulogy, or at least thought about it. Now you have an idea of how you'd describe your contribution at the end of your life. With that clarity, you'll start aligning the pieces and make them your reality. You'll look around at other people you relate to and admire. People who share the same values, are motivated by similar passions and abilities, and are focused on making the kind of impact that you care about. You can explore how they have built their brand and adopt similar traits or behaviors. You can even dress like them or follow their lead in some other way.

How do these individuals represent themselves? How do you represent yourself? Part of building a brand is showing up in a consistent way that builds trust and a good reputation. You want people to associate certain feelings, characteristics, and attributes with you. You do this through your actions, the words you speak, and the way you communicate your thoughts and feelings. You also do this by keeping your promises. In fact, the core of your brand, the basis of your reputation, are the promises you make and the promises you keep. If you tell someone you will do something, you do it. If you claim to care about something, your actions should show that. Actions speak louder than words, so make sure your behavior aligns with what you say about yourself and what you want people to say about you. The foundation of your legacy is built by you, with your words and your actions.

Part of building a brand is showing up in a consistent way that builds trust and a good reputation.

Are your actions congruent with your brand? If not, what do you need to start or stop doing to make sure you are aligned with how you want to be perceived?

Inspiring Others through How You Live

When I was in high school, I remember there was a girl whose name was Zephyr. She was a couple years older, but she left a lasting impression on me. There was something about her: she was always smiling and seemed to radiate a light wherever she went. She was popular and very pretty, but that's not what stuck out to me. What I remember about Zephyr was that despite her good looks and social status, she was always kind to anyone she came across. She was friendly with the cool people, and she warmly embraced and laughed with the less popular people. She was just a really nice person. In retrospect that is probably why she was so popular, but the way she carried herself had a big impact on me.

Years later, I sat down with my daughter Julia, who was ten and in the third grade. We were talking about popularity and being cool. I flashed back to high school and Zephyr. I told Julia that it was more important to be nice than to be popular, and that she should always make an effort to be kind and inclusive with everyone, whether they were deemed cool or not.

Julia took that advice to heart and was a very spirited elementary school student. To this day, she continues to make an effort to make people around her feel special and included, and she has earned the reputation of someone you want to be friends with. She walks into a room with a beaming smile and radiates positive energy, but more importantly, she is kind to everyone, and I couldn't be prouder.

Recently Julia shared with me how she had come across a girl who had to gone to elementary school with her—someone she didn't really remember—but the girl remembered Julia and told her how much it meant to her that when they were in school together, Julia always smiled at her and made her feel she had a friend. It had been hard for this girl, because at the time she was new to the school and felt shy and unsure of herself, but the fact that Julia made her feel seen had made all the difference for her.

Just think: I watched Zephyr in high school. Her kindness had such an impact on me that when I became a mother, I emphasized that very way of being with my adolescent daughter. She in turn absorbed the idea of being nice and through her kindness had a powerful impact on the people around her.

I'm telling you this story because each of us can inspire others through the way we live. We cannot underestimate how we lead by example. When others look to us to see how we act, it teaches more than our words ever will. When you live your life with intention and purpose, you will naturally inspire others. They will appreciate your conviction and authenticity and connect to you.

I guarantee that Zephyr didn't go through high school thinking that if she was kind to others, her influence would show up twenty years later and 200 miles away, but it did. I believe Julia too, through her leadership, will continue to have a positive influence on others.

Summary

Remember, your legacy is not just built on the "big things" you do or don't do in your life; it's made up of all the small choices you make on a daily basis. It's the little things like a wave, a hug, a moment of being fully present with your family, or sharing something that empowers someone else. It all matters, and it all makes a difference.

That's why it's so important to live with intention. You don't want to be a passive player in your life; you want every day to mean something. Set daily intentions and check in with yourself to make sure you're living each day in a way that reflects the woman you want to be remembered. This is a major part of living with purpose and designing your legacy. Each day counts, and every little gesture adds up. You get to define what legacy means to you. When you lead with your heart and stay true to your values, your life will speak for itself, not just in the moment, but for years to come. And it's uniquely yours.

Step Twelve
Design Your Legacy and Live Your Life with Purpose

Action Plan and Exercises

Set some time aside and go get your journal or the Accomplished Woman's Guide so you can apply these ideas to your life and take action with intention.

EXERCISE ONE: WRITE YOUR FUTURE EULOGY

This exercise is help you determine the legacy you want to leave behind. Create a vision of your life. Decide now what you want people to say about the way you lived your life, the people you affected, and what you will be remembered for. With this clarity, you can align your action with your vision, live your life with purpose, and determine your own legacy.

1. Write a future eulogy letter that describes the legacy you want to leave behind. What do you want people to say about you? Not just your accomplishments, but the way you made people feel, the values you represented, and how you showed up both personally and professionally.
2. What would that letter say if you had to write it today?
3. What are three things you need to change in order to align with the legacy you want to be known for?

EXERCISE TWO: HONORING YOUR CONTRIBUTIONS

This exercise will help you acknowledge the contributions you make in your life and how they build your legacy: the ones you make today, the ones you've made in the past, and the ones you hope to make in the future. It helps to look back at the choices you've made and connect those choices to an impact.

Fill in the chart below and list three items per section that are meaningful to you.

	Ways I contribute at home	Ways I contribute in the world (professionally or in the community)
Past		
Present		
Future		

EXERCISE THREE: LEADING THROUGH YOUR LEGACY

This exercise is intended to connect you to the importance of your leadership. Whether you lead with a capital L or a lower-case L, your actions impact others. The more intentional you are, the more powerful your impact will be.

Write down three ways you acted as a leader this past month, at home, at work, and in your community:

1.
2.
3.

What is one thing you can speak up about or share to empower someone else?

What knowledge or skill do you have from your experience that would have a positive impact on them?

EXERCISE FOUR: IMPACT AND INSPIRATION INVENTORY

The purpose of this exercise is to help you identify people who have inspired you, and how. You will also reflect on whom you might be inspiring, and how.

Answer the following questions:
1. Name three people who have inspired you.
2. What about them inspired you? How has your life been affected by them?
3. Who might be looking to you for inspiration?
4. What do you want to inspire in others?

EXERCISE FIVE: LIVING YOUR LEGACY

The purpose of this exercise is to keep you connected and intentional about living your life with purpose and staying in sync with what you want your legacy to be.

Journal about the following prompts:

What is one action I took last week that reflects my legacy?

How am I showing up for my family, my work, and myself? Is it aligned with my personal brand?

What is one area about which I want to be more intentional this week? What action will I take based on that intention?

Conclusion
You Are an Accomplished Woman

Throughout this book, it has been my main goal to help you see that you are already an accomplished woman. Each one of us achieves success in our own way. The secret is to clearly define success for yourself so that you know what it means to feel accomplished. That way, you can take steps every day to ensure that you see your success in the way live your life, the way you embrace your relationships, and the way you honor yourself as an amazing woman living an amazing life. Your life: designed by you.

This book has hopefully been a guide for you: the modern woman who is ready to live a life of purpose, balance, and fulfillment on her own terms. I have aimed to empower you to break free from outdated definitions of success and craft a vision that aligns with your unique values, passions, and priorities.

Together, we've gone through twelve important areas of your life and defined actionable steps in each one. Now let's explore each of those steps one more time to remind you of all that you've learned and empower you to use each tool in your life, starting now.

Step One:
Define Success for Yourself in Every Area of Your Life

Before you can set meaningful goals or build a life that reflects your values, you have to be clear about what success truly means to you. This step is about reflecting on your life, questioning where your beliefs come from, and redefining what it looks like to feel proud, accomplished, and fulfilled in all areas of your life, on your terms.

This step is important because your version of success is shaped by what you've absorbed from your past, your family, your culture, media, and other significant influences. We talked about the garden analogy and how those influences have planted beliefs in your garden, some of which are true for you and others are weeds that need to be plucked. Deconstruct your current narrative and determine how you define success for yourself: this is the only way you will stop working towards things that don't matter and start creating a life that feels authentic and aligned with what does.

Start by reflecting on your upbringing and the messages you absorbed about women, success, money, motherhood, relationships, and ambition. Think about what you were taught, which beliefs feel true for you now, and which beliefs you need to let go of because they no longer serve you.

For each area of your life, including career, finances, health, relationships, family, social impact, and personal growth, rewrite the script by asking yourself, "What does success look like to me? How do I measure it? What does it feel like? What would make me feel accomplished in this area?"

Step Two:
Determine What you Want to Have, Be, and Do and Set Goals in Every Area of Your Life

This step is about becoming crystal clear about what you want to have, be, or do in every area of your life. It's about designing your life by setting meaningful goals so that you live with purpose and intention. Without clear goals, you'll drift through life responding to the needs of others, feeling off balance, and never truly feeling satisfied with how you live.

Goals give purpose to your time and direction to your action. They make your efforts feel meaningful. When you are proactively working towards goals that are aligned with your values, you feel excited and engaged, and your life feels more fulfilling and accomplished. Daily goal setting is the key to claiming ownership of your time, because goals enable you to invest your time and energy in what matters most to you.

Goal setting is easy. Simply get a piece of paper and for each category of your life, write down what you want to have, be, or do in each area. Your goals should specific, measurable, time-bound and written in the positive, present tense. You got this! Set your targets and take action.

Step Three:
Build Your Self-Confidence, Recruit Resources to Help you Escape Your Comfort Zone, and Take Action

In this step, we worked on developing your self-confidence to help you overcome self-doubt and take action. We explored how the only way to live the life you want is to stop listening to those voices in your head that tell you, "You can't," "You shouldn't," or "You're not ready." There is so much possibility for you, and the way to access it is to escape the comfort zone. Go for it. Developing self-confidence and believing in yourself are the source of your momentum, and you have to move in order to go after the life you've envisioned for yourself.

We talked about learning to love yourself, with all of your quirks, and building your self-esteem by identifying the things you like about yourself and everything you are proud of. Let your inner cheerleader motivate you and keep you moving, one baby step at a time. She's the best friend in your head and believes in when you struggle.

Each time you act, you develop more confidence and feel more competent in your ability to meet your own needs and achieve your goals. With every success, you develop resilience. The more resilience you cultivate, the more unstoppable you become. You have to believe in yourself and trust that anything you want is possible.

Step Four:
Apply the Five C's in order to Communicate Clearly, Express Yourself, and Connect Authentically

This step is about learning how to express yourself and communicate clearly, confidently, and authentically. We discussed how clear communication enables you to meaningfully connect with others. Mutual understanding and appreciation build your personal and professional relationships. Your ability to communicate is the key to advocating for your needs, setting boundaries, fostering connection, and inspiring action.

We talked about the five C's of communication:

Components: the power of your words, impact of your tone, and nonverbal communication in your body language.

Consciousness: the importance of having self-awareness and knowing your thoughts and feelings in order to express yourself clearly and accurately understand others.

Construction: the art of framing your conversation, managing expectations, and setting yourself up for success in any exchange.

Collaboration: appreciating differences, setting boundaries, and seeking win-wins with others.

Consideration: the importance of appreciation, the power of a thank you, and the value of staying connected in your relationships and communications.

Step Five:
Identify Your Unique Value and Decide How to Use it

This step is about being able to recognize the unique gift you already have—your natural talent, strength, or skill—and connect it with your passion in order to give your actions a greater sense of purpose. When you identify what you are good at and what you care deeply about, you can use that clarity to make a meaningful impact in your home, work, or community. You can even start your own business. You experience greater personal fulfillment by using your talent with purpose.

First, identify your natural talent, or superpower, and then determine whom or what you are passionate about. When you find out where your skill and passion intersect, you can make your talent actionable. You can seize the opportunity to integrate it into your life. By doing this, you will experience a greater sense of purpose in all that you do.

Step Six:
Redefine what Success Means to you in Motherhood

This step tackles one of the most significant aspects of life for many women: motherhood, a period often under considered in traditional success models. We explored how it is a significant part of many women's lives and needs to be incorporated into one's vision of success. We worked to define what success in motherhood means to you and how to align your parenting goals with your personal values.

Additionally, we explored several techniques for being more present and fully showing up for your children, so you can cultivate connection and healthy relationships with them. We discussed how to balance ambition and family and talked about strategies to address challenges like time management, guilt, and self-care.

This step is about determining what motherhood means to you and what success would look like for you in this area, and then setting parenting goals and boundaries that enable you to be, and feel like, an accomplished mother.

Step Seven:
Build and Strengthen Relationships that Matter and Protect Yourself with Good Boundaries

Surrounding yourself with people who empower and support you and navigating the relationships that hold you back are a major key to success. The quality of your life is based on the quality of your relationships. No one achieves success alone. You need to invest in your relationships and cultivate those connections, not only to feel supported, but also to give your life additional meaning. You can earn all the money you can imagine, but without people you care about to share your time with, you might never feel satisfied.

In truth, a sense of unhappiness or distress in relationships makes it hard to focus to anything else. Often, we just hope things will work out on their own without realizing that relationships need to be nurtured with time and effort.

This step talked about how to build deeper connections and set strong boundaries. You can achieve more through collaboration and with a community that gives you a sense of belonging. We also talked about the importance of creating supportive personal and professional networks. Both contribute to your success, happiness, and fulfillment.

To cultivate meaningful relationships, use the **FRIENDS** framework:

Foster trust by being authentic and showing your vulnerability.

Respect others by honoring boundaries and accepting differences.

Invest time to help the relationship develop and grow.

Express gratitude to make people feel important and appreciated.

Navigate conflict with consideration so people feel seen, heard, and validated.

Develop mutual respect and encourage others to be the best version of themselves.

Share experiences and create memories with the people you care about.

To set boundaries with tricky people, use the **BOLD** method:
Be clear about what you need in the situation.
Openly and directly communicate with assertiveness.
Listen for their response, and be prepared to restate your boundary.
Defend your needs kindly but firmly. Don't give in.

Step Eight:
Prioritize Your Health and Well-Being

Your health and well-being are the foundation for success. Without health, you cannot achieve your goals or balance your many responsibilities. We explored several ways for you to prioritize your health and protect your well-being so you can show up to the best of your ability and accomplish the tasks that matter to you.

We talked about the significance of stress and how it affects your focus, your relationships, and your ability to perform. You learned stress management techniques and how to set boundaries to protect your energy and well-being.

The goal of this step is to highlight the fact that you have to take your health seriously and prioritize your mental and physical well-being. You are important. Your state of mental, physical, and emotional health makes it either possible or impossible for you to be an accomplished woman.

Step Nine:
Improve Your Relationship with Money and Take Action to Feel Financially Empowered

This step was about transforming your relationship with money in every way—emotionally, mentally, and practically—so you feel more confident and in control of your financial life. We explored the importance of having a good relationship with money. We also saw how everyone develops a script at a young age that influences how they feel and handle money. We talked about the messages you grew up with and how they shape your behavior. You may associate money with control or love: maybe you grew up always wanting or needing money, so an attitude of abundance is hard for you to adopt. We explored how money is a loaded topic for most people, especially women, who have been shaped by cultural messages and unhealthy money dynamics.

I know it may seem hard to go from feeling stuck, disempowered, or confused about money to a place of security, confidence, and financial ownership, but you can do it! Take ownership of your finances by knowing your numbers, tracking your spending, and setting clear financial goals. Money habits are like any other habits. Decide what beliefs you want to adopt, the relationship with it you want to have, and then align your actions with those values.

Step Ten: Master Your Time, Stay Focused and Live a Balanced Life

For you to feel balanced and grounded, your actions have to reflect what matters to you. You have to decide where you want to invest your time and energy, and then you need to be proactive in implementing your decisions. We talked about the importance of planning in advance. I suggested a wall calendar, a weekly planner, or any other mode that works for you. You will be happier and more productive in your use of time if you organize your tasks, navigate obstacles, make sure you do what you need to do, and stay focused.

In this way, you can avoid feeling guilty about the way you spend your time.

Self-discipline and motivation have to do with knowing what drives you—the carrot or the stick—and reminding yourself of why your actions have meaning so you can stay committed and carry through. The more in control you feel of your time, the more you can show up for the people and priorities in your life.

Step Eleven:
Commit to being a Lifelong Learner

This step is about choosing to be a lifelong learner and a student of your own experiences, relationships, and the world around you. You don't have to stop learning and growing when you finish school; in fact, you should commit to learning and staying engaged at every phase of your life. When you keep learning, you keep evolving, which makes you feel excited about life. Novelty gives you confidence and enthusiasm as you navigate your ever-evolving experiences. Knowledge and understanding of what's going on around you in a deeper way makes you feel more empowered. But if you stop learning, you stop living, and life can start to feel stagnant and boring. When you commit to your own continual growth, you stay inspired and bring meaning and joy into your everyday experience.

Step Twelve:
Design Your Legacy and Live a Meaningful Life

We concluded this process with defining the legacy you want to leave. In this way, you give deeper meaning to your actions and make decisions based on how you want to be remembered. This awareness can transform your approach to everything from parenting and leadership to everyday conversations and commitments.

You get to intentionally design your legacy, and that legacy isn't created only by big achievements, but also by your small, daily choices. It's the way you treat others and how you show up in your relationships, your work, and your community. You are a leader in your life and an example to others. Never underestimate the power of a smile, the gift of knowledge, or the value of your undivided attention.

Think about what kind of impact you want to leave and how can you inspire others. You live your legacy every day. Decide what you want it to look like and fully step in to yourself.

And there we have it: twelve steps to redefine success and live life on your own terms. Take these steps and apply these ideas in your life, embracing all that you are, have, and do—you, the accomplished woman.

About the Author

DR. CHRISTINA TRACY STEIN is a Licensed Marriage and Family therapist, clinical sexologist, business coach, and international speaker who has spent nearly two decades helping individuals and couples create passionate, authentic, and successful lives. She is known for blending practical psychology with timeless success principles, guiding her clients and audiences to deepen connection, communicate with clarity, and live in alignment with their deepest values.

As the daughter of legendary success expert Brian Tracy, Christina grew up immersed in the science of achievement—and brings a fresh, feminine perspective to what it means to be accomplished today. She has co-authored three books on personal and professional development, including the international bestseller *Kiss That Frog!*, which has sold over 300,000 copies worldwide.

Through private sessions, workshops, and speaking engagements across the U.S., Europe, and Asia, Christina equips ambitious women, couples, and entrepreneurs with step-by-step tools to improve communication, strengthen relationships, and redefine success on their own terms. *The Accomplished Woman* is the culmination of her work, offering a proven path to clarity, confidence, and purpose—so women can create a life that feels as good on the inside as it looks on the outside.

Christina lives in Santa Monica, California with her husband and three children. She loves traveling, walking with her two dogs, and collecting crystals and other metaphysical treasures.

Work with Dr. Christina Tracy Stein

You've just finished *The Accomplished Woman*—now it's time to take everything you've learned and apply it to your own life. Here's how we can work together:

The Accomplished Woman: Your Next Evolution

A private coaching journey to help you redefine success and create a life you truly love. This 12-session program is designed for women ready to reconnect with their true desires, build confidence, strengthen relationships, reclaim time and energy, and live in alignment with their deepest values. Together, we'll create your Success Manifesto, set purposeful goals, and design a life that feels balanced, inspired, and uniquely yours.

The Accomplished Couple

A proven 12-session coaching experience to reignite passion and connection. Perfect for couples ready to rebuild emotional intimacy, improve communication, and navigate challenges as a team. You'll learn practical tools to keep love alive, manage stress together, and create rituals that bring joy and playfulness back into your relationship. Whether you want to strengthen a good relationship or repair a struggling one, this program offers a step-by-step path to a thriving partnership.

The Accomplished Entrepreneur

Turn your expertise and life experience into a thriving business. This transformational program will help you define your niche, craft your signature framework, and develop both a low-ticket offer and a high-ticket signature program. You'll learn to build a powerful personal brand, deliver a compelling keynote, and design a one-year marketing plan that sets you up for growth. If you're ready to step into thought leadership and turn your passion into profit, this program is for you. Your Next Step Your journey doesn't have to end with the last page of this book. Schedule a complimentary consultation to explore which program is right for you and take the next step toward creating the life, relationship, or business you truly desire.

Your Next Step

Your journey doesn't have to end with the last page of this book. Schedule a complimentary consultation to explore which program is right for you and take the next step toward creating the life, relationship, or business you truly desire.

Connect at: drchristinatracystein.com
Facebook: Dr. Christina Tracy Stein
Instagram: @drchristinatracystein

Don't forget to download your free guide at
www.theaccomplishedwomanguide.com